Deadly Indifference

Eric Sammons

D E A D L Y
INDIFFERENCE

How the Church Lost Her Mission
and How We Can Reclaim It

CRISIS
PUBLICATIONS

Manchester, New Hampshire

Crisis Publications
Box 5284, Manchester, NH 03108
1-800-888-9344

www.CrisisMagazine.com

paperback ISBN 978-1-64413-250-0

ebook ISBN 978-1-64413-251-7

Library of Congress Control Number: 2021934488

First printing

To my children,
Anna, Lucy, Maria, Peter,
Hope, Madeline, and Lydia,
with their peers, the next generation
to defend and proclaim the truth
and beauty of the Faith

Contents

Foreword

The essence of the mission of the Church coincides with the mission of Jesus Christ, the Eternal Word of God, the Second Person of the Holy Trinity, who became man, and who confessed, "For this I was born, and for this I have come into the world, to bear witness to the truth. Every one who is of the truth hears my voice" (John 18:37). And so the Church of all times and in all times spoke and should speak likewise, "For this purpose Christ, the Eternal Truth, founded me and for this purpose I lived and will live in this world—to bear witness to the truth." These words the pope and every bishop and priest of our day should speak.

Indeed, in our day war is almost everywhere stirred up and fomented against the revealed truth of God and against the primary mission of the Church to proclaim it strenuously and unambiguously. A little more than one hundred years ago Pope Pius X presented us a realistic view of a widespread indifference as a characteristic feature of the modern time. The following adequate portrayal given by this holy pontiff is fully applicable to our time:

> [A] sacrilegious war ... is now, almost everywhere, stirred up and fomented against God. For in truth, "The nations

have raged and the peoples imagined vain things" (Ps. 2:1) against their Creator, so frequent is the cry of the enemies of God: "Depart from us" (Job 21:14). And as might be expected we find extinguished among the majority of men all respect for the Eternal God, and no regard paid in the manifestations of public and private life to the Supreme Will—nay, every effort and every artifice is used to destroy utterly the memory and the knowledge of God....

We shall never, however much we exert ourselves, succeed in calling men back to the majesty and empire of God, except by means of Jesus Christ. "No one," the Apostle admonishes us, "can lay other foundation than that which has been laid, which is Jesus Christ" (1 Cor. 3:11). It is Christ alone "whom the Father sanctified and sent into this world" (Isa. 10:36), "the splendor of the Father and the image of His substance" (Heb. 1:3), true God and true man: without whom nobody can know God with the knowledge for salvation, "neither doth anyone know the Father but the Son, and he to whom it shall please the Son to reveal Him" (Matt. 11:27). Hence it follows that to restore all things in Christ and to lead men back to submission to God is one and the same aim ...

The times we live in demand action—but action which consists entirely in observing with fidelity and zeal the divine laws and the precepts of the Church, in the frank and open profession of religion, in the exercise of every kind of charitable works, without regard to selfinterest or worldly advantage. Such luminous examples given by the great army of soldiers of Christ will be of much greater avail in moving and drawing men than words and sublime dissertations ... Oh! when in every city and village the law of the Lord is faithfully observed, when respect is shown for sacred things, when the Sacraments are frequented, and the ordinances of Christian life fulfilled ... it will also contribute largely to temporal welfare and the advantage of human society ... it will be clear to all that the Church, such as it was instituted by Christ, must enjoy full and entire liberty and independence from all foreign dominion. (*E supremi*, October 4, 1903, 4; 8; 14)

Cardinal Louis Pie, a great nineteenth-century bishop and confessor of the Catholic Faith in France, left us the following valid and timely exhortation to guard ourselves from a deadly indifference, the main spiritual sickness of our time, and to combat it at the same time with the spiritual means God bestowed us in His holy Church:

When you are condemned to see the triumph of the evil, you should never acclaim, you should never say to the evil: you are good; you should never say to the decadence: you are the progress; you should never say to the night: you are the light; you should never say to the death: you are the life. Sanctify yourselves in the time in which God has placed you; deplore the evils and the disorders, which God tolerates; oppose to them the energy of your works and of your efforts, your whole life pure from errors, free from the evil works, so that after the life here on earth you will be one with the Spirit of the Lord, you will be admitted to be one with the Lord, for as Saint Paul said: "He who is joined to the Lord becomes one spirit with him" (1 Cor. 6:17). (From the last sermon of Cardinal Pie, bishop of Poitiers, on 18 May 1880)

The present work of Eric Sammons, *Deadly Indifference: How the Church Lost Her Mission and How We Can Reclaim It*, is a valuable tool to open one's eyes to the true state of the spiritual disease in the life of the Church, which must be rightly diagnosed as a deadly indifferentism towards the revealed and unchangeable truths. At the same time, the merit of this book consists in showing the true ecclesiastic spirit of a supernatural love and respect towards the Church, an attitude which should lead everyone who is deeply concerned and who does not simply bury his head in the sand to recognize the undeniable fact of the spiritual pandemic raging in the life of the Church. The following words of Eric Sammons are in this sense enlightening and encouraging: "Any criticism a Catholic levels against a pope or a council should be offered carefully and in humility. No one wants to criticize his mother; he wants the world always to be like it was when he was a young child, where mom was always right and all-knowing. Yet that's not realistic in this fallen world. We should not enjoy criticizing Church leaders, but we must do so at times in order that she may fulfill her glorious mission."

May this book have a wide and beneficial reach and with God's grace enkindle in the minds and hearts of its readers an unshakable love for the truth and the Church, because in her as St. Augustine says, "instead of victory, is truth; instead of high rank, holiness; instead of peace, felicity; instead of life, eternity." (*Civ* 15:1)

+ Athanasius Schneider
Auxiliary Bishop of the Archdiocese
of Saint Mary in Astana
January 28, 2021

Deadly Indifference

Introduction

The Catholic Church is in crisis. As much as bishops and priests love to talk about their "vibrant" and "dynamic" dioceses and parishes, most people recognize this as propaganda the likes of which would make the editors of Soviet-era *Pravda* blush. The numbers show anything but vibrancy and dynamism.

In America, there are so many former Catholics that this group makes up the second largest "religion." Fewer than 25 percent of self-identifying American Catholics attend Mass weekly.

Consider sacramental life: In the past fifty years, the number of Catholic infant Baptisms in this country has dropped by over 45 percent while the overall U.S. population has increased by more than 60 percent. The number of Catholic priests has decreased by 40 percent (and the number of religious sisters has decreased by a staggering 74 percent). Marriages are down 68 percent since 1970.[1] The typical parish today likely has a few dozen people at most receive the sacrament of Confession each week. Compare

---

[1] "Frequently Requested Church Statistics," Center for Applied Research in the Apostolate, https://cara.georgetown.edu/ frequently-requested-church-statistics/.

that to a New York parish that heard more than 78,000 confessions in a single year back in the 1890s.[2]

Not long ago I attended a city-wide men's Eucharistic procession. The organizers were pleased that more than three hundred men attended. However, this same procession was held here in the 1930s and 1940s with more than fifty thousand men each year attending. The local Major League Baseball stadium had to be rented out just to fit everyone for the closing Benediction! Now we're happy if we half-fill a parish church.

Other extra-sacramental activities fare no better: any parish volunteer today can tell stories about the difficulty of getting parishioners to show up for Bible studies, charitable outreaches, or education classes. Usually it's the same ten people at every event. Most parish members don't have time to dedicate more than an hour a week (or less) to the parish.

Far from what could be called "vibrant," living as a Catholic today has become *beige*. A Catholic American is indistinguishable from any other American. How he lives and what he believes is more determined by his class than by his religion. His Catholicism has little impact on his daily life.

Again, the Catholic Church is in crisis. And if she doesn't take steps to reverse these troubling trends and become impactful again, she will eventually be no more than a cultural relic of the past, long forgotten in the minds of future generations. Of course, we know Christ promised that the gates of Hell shall not prevail against the Church (cf. Matt. 16:18), but this promise does not guarantee that pockets of the Church — even large pockets — will not disappear. We need only look at Northern

---

[2] James O'Toole, "Hear No Evil," *Boston College Magazine*, Fall 2000, https://bcm.bc.edu/issues/fall_2000/features.html.

Africa after the Muslim invasions or England after Henry VIII to know that Catholicism can essentially disappear from large geographic areas. We cannot presume that the Church will not significantly diminish, even disappear, in America and the Western world.

So, how did this happen, and what can be done? Catholics have been debating this for decades, struggling to determine how we got here and the path forward. But too often we're like a dog chasing his tail, debating what teachings are or are not infallible and what aspects of the Faith have or have not changed. Could it be that the roots of our problem are more insidious than that? Perhaps they're not to be found in a single document, a single council, or a single change. Perhaps the roots are much more extensive than that.

In this book, I argue that *religious indifference* has permeated the Church in almost every aspect of her life and ministry. The idea that in the long run one's religion doesn't much matter has taken root in the Church—an idea fostered by the words and actions of our leaders and quickly adopted by our members.

Religious indifference is the fruit of Religious Pluralism: the belief that there is no one true religion; that many or perhaps all religions teach truth and are capable of leading someone to salvation. If multiple religions, perhaps even all religions, are valid and can lead someone to Heaven, then why do their differences matter? One can be indifferent to them. Religious indifference looks at various religions and essentially says, "The end result of each is the same."

This indifference is deadly to Catholicism in two ways: first, it saps the missionary spirit of the Church. And second, it weakens the attachments Catholics have to the Church, eventually leaving them with no reason to stick around. In effect, religious indifference attacks both the desire to gain new members and the desire of existing members to remain.

The indifference that reigns in the Church shocked me when I first converted to Catholicism in the early 1990s. Part of what had attracted me to Catholicism was the historical passion of its members. Countless Catholics over the centuries faced hardships, torture, and even death for their faith, and they held onto that faith like the precious pearl it is. Great missionary saints through the centuries eagerly traveled the world to bring people to Christ: St. Augustine of Canterbury traveling to England, Sts. Cyril and Methodius preaching to the Slavs, St. Francis of Assisi trying to convert the Islamic Sultan, St. Francis Xavier baptizing count-less people, and St. Isaac Jogues enduring torture to bring the Gospel to the Native Americans. These heroic saints believed with all their heart that Catholicism was the One True Faith and that it needed to be spread to the ends of the earth. These stories stirred my Evangelical Protestant heart. I assumed that Catholics, who have the fullness of the Faith and a history of proclaiming and defending it, must be excited about their faith and want to share it with others.

Yet after I became Catholic I was surprised at the extent to which this kind of missionary spirit was actually discouraged. The idea that a Catholic should urge a non-Catholic to convert was offensive to many inside the Church. At the very least, most Catholics just didn't see the point: Why bother? After all, most religions are good and most people are likely going to Heaven. The modern Catholic was called to "dialogue" with non-Catho-lics in order to make this world a better place, not try to convert them to help them in the world to come. What's more, millions of Catholics were indifferent to their own practice of the Faith, and many of them were dropping out altogether.

So what happened? How did the Church go from being full of Catholics who were sure of their faith and wanted to share it with others, to what we have today—widespread indifference?

In this book I will argue that a major shift in emphasis inside the Church began in earnest in the 1960s and led to a radical change in how Catholics perceive their religion. This Emphasis Shift impacted all aspects of Church life and led to a diminishment of the missions and an exodus of members. I will detail how that Emphasis Shift occurred, and how it still impacts the Church today. But I will also include a path forward: a way to overcome the prevailing religious indifference and help Catholics regain confidence in their religion. While the story I tell in this book is a tragic one, I'm hopeful that by understanding this tragedy we can recover what was lost and again be a light to a darkened world.

I. Church Teaching on Salvation

If I say the Church has lost sight of her mission, I'm implying that there was a time when we had a good handle on it. If we start at the beginning, we cannot doubt that the apostles knew what their mission was and pursued it straight to martyrdom. We see this same firmness of purpose in the first Christians, the monastic fathers of the early Middle Ages, the mendicants and crusaders of the later Middle Ages, and the conquerors of the post-Reformation period.

These men and women knew what the Church's mission was. Do we? In this section we will uncover the mission of the Church and explore how that mission shaped the Church's perception of herself.

A warning to the reader, however: the full implications of the mission of the Church might be startling. Most Catholics have never heard it, even those who have attended Mass their whole lives. And that is the point of this book: the Church's mission and all that it entails has been forgotten. So before we go about finding out *how* it was lost, let's get our bearings and understand the Church's mission and the practical implications it had in the course of the Church's history.

1

What Is the Mission of the Church?

A few years ago I stood watching my young daughter in the back yard. She was walking around, head bent toward the ground, clearly searching for something. When I asked what she was looking for, she replied, "I don't know, I'm just trying to help Peter [her older brother] find it."

One of the claims I make in this book is that the Church has lost sight of her mission. But before we look at how this happened, it's important to know what that mission is. Otherwise, we'll be like my daughter, wandering around without any clue what we're looking for.

An understanding of the Church's mission impacts every facet of the Church's life, from the actions of the Supreme Pontiff, the pope, to the faith life of the most humble parishioner. If, for example, the primary mission of the Church is to help the poor, then the focus of the work of the pope and bishops will be to institute charities and to work for political change that favors those less fortunate. Further, each Catholic's spiritual life will center around service to the poor. If, on the other hand, the Church's mission is to provide a social community in which members are supported and nourished, then the focus of parish life, for example, will be to host activities for members to interact and get to know one another. The Church's mission determines the practical life of the Church and all her members at all levels.

So what is the Church's mission?

One place we can discover the Church's mission might be surprising: the *Code of Canon Law*. This code is typically seen as a dry legal document only of concern to Church officials and canon lawyers. However, the very last canon in the code reveals something very important. It states, "the salvation of souls ... must always be the supreme law" (Can. 1752). In other words, the "supreme law" that governs all the rules—and the entire institution, in fact—is the salvation of souls. Even though the Church is a visible institution and therefore needs laws to operate properly (more than 1,750 of them!), all these laws serve that one purpose.

The *Catechism of the Catholic Church* (CCC) further develops this theme. It states that "As the 'convocation' of all men for salvation, the Church in her very nature is missionary, sent by Christ to all the nations to make disciples of them" (CCC 767). It also calls the Church the "sacrament of salvation" (CCC 780); the means by which people are saved. Or, as the old *Baltimore Catechism* states plainly, "Christ founded the Church to bring all men to eternal salvation."[3]

This, then, is the very purpose of the Church's entire existence, her mission in this world: the salvation of souls. Even while the Church is involved in social welfare projects, or the political order, or economic reforms, her primary mission to lead people to Heaven remains. Christ himself gave the Church this mandate when He told the apostles right before His Ascension,

---

[3] Bennet Kelley, C.P., *Saint Joseph Baltimore Catechism No. 2* (New York: Catholic Book Publishing Co, 1962), Question 138.

"Go therefore and make disciples of all nations, baptizing them in the name of the Father and of the Son and of the Holy Spirit, teaching them to observe all that I have commanded you" (Matt. 28:19-20). Christ didn't command the apostles to make the world a better place, or even to help the poor (although those things are laudable), He commanded they *make disciples*—and the purpose of being a disciple of Christ is eventually to spend eternity with Him in Heaven.

So we see that the Church's mission is to save souls. But answering the first question raises another one: How? How are souls saved? Is salvation found by being a good person? Or maybe it entails accepting a certain set of beliefs. Or perhaps it's a combination of these and other things. The words of Christ that we just read point to the answer. In order to make disciples who will be saved, the apostles were to do two things: *baptize* and *teach*. In other words, to be a disciple you must become a member of Christ's Body, the Church (that's what Baptism accomplishes), and also stay in that Church by following the teachings of Christ. Thus, *membership in the Church is necessary for salvation*. The ramifications of this truth cannot be overestimated; we'll see in this book that this is the Church's historic understanding of her mission: she is here to save souls, and only through the Church can souls be saved.

I will argue that, by forgetting this second point—that salvation comes through membership in the Church—Catholics have forgotten the first point: the Church's mission is to save souls. Only by recovering a sense of the necessity of the Church will we be able to reclaim the Church's mission.

2

"Outside the Church There Is No Salvation"

Today we live in a religiously diverse society. It's not uncommon for a Catholic to have a Protestant relative, a Muslim neighbor, or a Jewish co-worker (or perhaps all three). Any Catholic under the age of sixty has likely never heard a Church leader criticize a non-Catholic belief system. It's likely, in fact, that the average Catholic today sees Catholicism as just one option among many legitimate religions; i.e., he holds to the belief system known as Religious Pluralism.

Yet this was not always the case. In fact, until the 1960s, the idea of Religious Pluralism was literally anathema among Catholics. Instead, the average Catholic accepted that membership in the Catholic Church was necessary for salvation and that non-Catholics were in serious danger of going to Hell. Because of this, Catholics knew that the core mission of the Church was to convert people to Catholicism so that they could be saved from eternal damnation. Leaving the Church was largely unthinkable.

The Church's traditional doctrine on salvation and the role of other religions can be summed up in the famous Latin phrase, *extra Ecclesiam nulla salus* (EENS), which means "outside the Church there is no salvation." Although this teaching has been tucked away in a back closet by Church leaders like an embarrassing relic of the past, it has a long, venerable history and is still the official teaching of the Church. If hearing the phrase "outside the Church there is no salvation" immediately elicits in your mind the response "But what about ... " I kindly ask you to hold that thought—we'll get to that. But don't forget that reaction, because you're helping me make my argument.

Where then did this "rigid" belief regarding the uniqueness of the Catholic Church come from and what does it mean? What are its origins? That's what we're going to explore in this chapter.

You Shall Have No Other Gods before Me

Tracing the roots of Catholicism to ancient Judaism, we find there the foundations of EENS. If you had to sum up the Old Testament in one sentence, you could say that it is the history of God asking His people to be faithful to Him and their failure to do so. After God rescues His people from slavery in Egypt, He wants them to be set apart from the rest of the nations, to be an example to them. He gives to Moses Ten Commandments to form the basis of this new people. The very first commandment makes clear what is most important: "You shall have no other gods before me" (Exod. 20:3). This commandment is immediately followed by further, practical commands as well as the consequences if this command is broken:

> You shall not make for yourself a graven image, or any likeness of anything that is in heaven above, or that is in the earth beneath, or that is in the water under the earth; you shall not bow down to them or serve them; for I the LORD your God am a jealous God, visiting the iniquity of the fathers upon the children to the third and the fourth generation of those who hate me, but showing steadfast

love to thousands of those who love me and keep my
commandments. (Exod. 20:4-6)

The idea of God as "a jealous God" recurs throughout the
Old Testament. It's easy to misinterpret what this means. God
isn't like a controlling boyfriend with an irrational fear that if
his girlfriend leaves her apartment she'll meet someone else.
God is "jealous" in the sense that He knows what each person
is made for: communion with Him. He is jealous for our souls
and demands that we dedicate ourselves only to Him. Unlike
the jealous boyfriend's wishes, God's desire for us also "happens"
to be what will give us true happiness.

The first commandment, then, is the foundation of the other
commandments, as well as the foundation of the entire religion
of Judaism and the nation of ancient Israel: *you cannot worship
other gods!* Sadly, though, we see in the Old Testament that time
and time again this is exactly what Israel does.

In the two books of Kings, which tell the story of the long
downfall of Israel after the death of King David, the sacred authors narrate a recurring theme: a king who is faithful to God
has a good reign, but one who allows the worship of false gods
in the land does not. (It's important to remember that there
was no concept of a "separation of Church and State" in ancient Israel. Politics and religion were deeply intertwined, and
flawed religious practices were understood to lead to significant
political problems.) After the Jewish Kingdom divides into the
Northern Kingdom (Israel) and the Southern Kingdom (Judah)
following the death of King Solomon, succeeding kings are
described as either doing "right in the sight of the Lord" or doing "what was evil in the sight of the Lord." And the sole basis
of determining whether a king is doing "right" or "what was

evil" is their embrace of other religions in the land. The more a king tolerates other religions, the more evil he is considered. After all, any worship of a false god is a violation of the first, and most important, commandment to have no other gods before the Lord God.

An unsettling incident found in 2 Kings 10 shows how far the sacred author believes kings should go to keep the first commandment. The worship of the false god Baal is prevalent in the Northern Kingdom of Israel in the ninth century B.C. King Ahab, reigning from 874-853 B.C., fosters the religion of Baal. After King Jehu (841-814) comes to the throne of Israel, he assembles all the people and announces, "Ahab served Baal a little; but Jehu will serve him much. Now therefore call to me all the prophets of Baal, all his worshipers and all his priests; let none be missing, for I have a great sacrifice to offer to Baal; whoever is missing shall not live" (2 Kings 10:18-19). But it's a trick. Although it appears at first that Jehu is continuing this false religion, the sacred author tells us, "Jehu did it with cunning in order to destroy the worshipers of Baal" (2 Kings 10:19). Jehu gathers all the worshipers of Baal together, and he has them slaughtered and the pillar and house of Baal destroyed.

Some biblical commentators would simply say that this violent incident should be interpreted as something God permitted, but did not endorse, much like the widespread polygamy found among the ancient Israelites. Yet, unlike in the case of polygamy, the Bible itself says that King Jehu's actions were righteous: "And the LORD said to Jehu, 'Because *you have done well in carrying out what is right in my eyes*, and have done to the house of Ahab according to all that was in my heart, your sons of the fourth generation shall sit on the throne of Israel'" (2 Kings 10:30, emphasis added).

Does this mean that Catholics today should be wiping out people who follow other religions? Obviously not. But this passage should make us pause and reflect on the importance of the first commandment and practicing right religion. Nowhere in the Old Testament is Religious Pluralism endorsed, and in fact, it is repeatedly and harshly condemned. The view of ancient Judaism when it comes to other religions is summed up in Wisdom 14:27: "For the worship of idols ... is the beginning and cause and end of every evil."

No Other Name

But that's the Old Testament; don't things change with the New Testament? Yes and no. It's important to remember that the first Christians do not see themselves as founding a new religion; instead, they believe following Jesus Christ is the *fulfillment* of Judaism. So although many of the ritual practices are modified or even jettisoned, fundamental beliefs are retained, including a dogged devotion to the first commandment. However, with the advent of the God-Man, the exclusivist attitude regarding religion Christians had held as Jews is "transferred," so to speak, to Jesus Christ.

Jesus Himself declares that salvation comes through Him, saying to the Apostles, "I am the way, and the truth, and the life; no one comes to the Father, but by me" (John 14:6). The first Christians make it clear that Jesus was the *only* way to salvation. In the first days of the Church, St. Peter boldly proclaims about Jesus, "there is salvation in no one else, for there is no other name under heaven given among men by which we must be saved" (Acts 4:12).

The writings of St. Paul are also infused with this assumption—that it is necessary for all people to convert to Christ and, further, to join His Body, the Church, in order to be with Him forever in Heaven. He writes to Timothy of Christ's unique role in the salvation of men: "God our Savior ... desires all men to be saved and to come to the knowledge of the truth. For there is one God, and there is one mediator between God and men, the man Christ Jesus" (1 Tim. 2:3-5). And for Paul, as for all the early Christians, to receive salvation in Christ it is necessary to be part of the Body of Christ, the Church.

Paul's close connection between Christ and the Church is based on the experience of his conversion. Before his conversion, Paul was persecuting the Church, but when at his conversion he asks who is speaking to him, he hears, "I am Jesus, whom you are persecuting" (Acts 9:5). Paul hears the Lord say that by persecuting the Church, he is persecuting Jesus, and that message stuck with him his entire life. When Paul says that *Christ* is necessary for salvation, he is also saying that *the Church* is necessary for salvation.

The Early Church

The early Christians, then, are no religious Pluralists; they believe that Christ is the only means of salvation, and further, that membership in the Church is the only way to be united to Christ and receive His salvation. This attitude is in stark contrast to the Roman world around them. Ancient Rome was famously tolerant regarding religion. One can believe whatever he wants, as long as he also acknowledges the Roman gods. Yet the early Christians refuse to do so. Even offering a small pinch of incense to the false Roman gods is idolatry—the very violation of the first commandment for which the ancient Israelites were condemned. The Church, from her foundations, was intolerant toward the practice of other religions.

This exclusive attitude came to be summarized in the phrase *extra Ecclesiam nulla salus*—outside the Church there is no salvation. The first known instance of EENS is attributed to St. Cyprian of Carthage, a Church Father of the third century, although the idea is found in even earlier Christian writings. A second-century Church Father, St. Irenaeus, for example, wrote that the Church is the "door of life."[4] Over time, the exclusive nature of the Church—that the Church is the *only* way to salvation—becomes more prominent in the teachings of Catholic saints, theologians, and councils. St. Augustine writes, "No man can find salvation except in the Catholic Church."[5] The Athanasian Creed, an influential creed written in the late fifth/early sixth century, opens with "Whosoever will be saved, before all things it is necessary that he hold the catholic faith." Many Church Fathers, including St. Cyprian, St. Jerome, and St. Augustine, compare the Church to the Ark of Noah, outside of which one cannot be saved.

Similar to King Jehu of ancient Israel, the early Christians do not believe it is possible to compromise with non-Christian religions. Since Christianity is the only way to Heaven, and membership in the Church is the only way to be a Christian, the most loving thing a Christian can do is to work for the end of non-Christian religions and to urge non-Christians to convert to the Church.

Institutionalizing EENS

In the medieval Church, the teaching that "outside the Church there is no salvation" becomes officially enshrined as popes and councils make EENS a binding part of the Faith. In 1215, the Fourth Lateran Council teaches, "There is indeed one universal church of the faithful, outside of which nobody at all is saved."[6]

---

4   St. Irenaeus, *Against Heresies*, bk. 3, chap. 4.
5   St. Augustine, *Sermo ad Caesariensis Ecclesia plebem*, 6.
6   Lateran Council IV, Constitution 1.

Pope Boniface VIII in 1302 writes in the encyclical *Unam Sanctam*, "Urged by faith, we are obliged to believe and to maintain that the Church is one, holy, catholic, and also apostolic. We believe in her firmly and we confess with simplicity that outside of her there is neither salvation nor the remission of sins." In 1442, the Council of Florence declares, "It [the holy Roman church] firmly believes, professes and preaches that all those who are outside the catholic church, not only pagans but also Jews or heretics and schismatics, cannot share in eternal life and will go into the everlasting fire which was prepared for the devil and his angels, unless they are joined to the catholic church before the end of their lives."[7] The medieval Catholic assumes that if you want eternal salvation, you need to be Catholic.

In the nineteenth century, this belief is still being proclaimed by the Church and held by the faithful. Pope Pius IX declares in 1854, "For, it must be held by faith that outside the Apostolic Roman Church, no one can be saved; that this is the only ark of salvation; that he who shall not have entered therein will perish in the flood."[8] Nine years later, the same pope notes,

> Here we must again mention and reprove a most serious error in which some Catholics have unhappily fallen, thinking that men living in errors and altogether apart from the true faith and Catholic unity can attain to eternal life. This indeed is completely opposed to Catholic doctrine.... It is also a perfectly well known Catholic dogma that no one can be saved outside the Catholic Church.[9]

7 Session 11.
8 Pope Pius IX, Allocution *Singulari Quadam* (December 8, 1854).
9 Pope Pius IX, *Quanto Conficiamur Moerore*, 7-8.

Then in 1870, Catholic bishops gather from around the world for the First Vatican Council. One of their objectives is to promulgate a dogmatic constitution including a statement on the necessity of the Church for salvation. Planners of the council create a *schema* to be used as a template for drafting the constitution. It states, "Moreover it is a dogma of faith, that no one can be saved outside the church."[10] However, due to the outbreak of the Franco-Prussian war, Vatican I is halted before the Council fathers can finalize and promulgate the constitution.

The Church in the first half of the twentieth century continues to insist on the truth of EENS. Pope Pius XII in 1943 writes, "Those who do not belong to the visible Body of the Catholic Church ... We ask each and every one of them to correspond to the interior movements of grace, and to seek to withdraw from that state in which they cannot be sure of their salvation."[11] And in 1949 the Sacred Congregation of the Holy Office issues a letter stating, "Among those things which the Church has always preached and will never cease to preach is contained also that infallible statement by which we are taught that there is no salvation outside the Church."[12]

Of all the teachings of the Catholic Church, few have been taught more consistently throughout her history than *extra Ecclesiam nulla salus.*

---

[10] Quoted in Francis Sullivan, *Salvation Outside the Church?* (New York: Paulist Press, 1992), 120.

[11] Pope Pius XII, *Mystici Corporis Christi*, 103.

[12] Supreme Sacred Congregation of the Holy Office, *Suprema haec sacra* (August 8, 1949).

3

Proclaiming the Only Ark of Salvation

What is the practical impact of *extra Ecclesiam nulla salus*? Most Catholics today are unaware of this dogma, but throughout the history of the Church, it has had a profound impact on how Catholics view the Church, salvation, and the status of non-Catholic religions. The two greatest consequences EENS has had in the life of the Church are as the driving force behind her missionary efforts and in setting Catholics apart from the rest of the world.

Missionary Drive

Although Christianity was birthed in Judaism, Christians have always held a fundamentally different attitude toward missionary activity than the ancient Jews. While ancient Judaism saw itself as an example for other nations without necessarily reaching out to convert them, Christianity from the beginning has been a missionary faith. The final words of Christ recorded in the Gospel of Matthew are the foundation of that missionary spirit: "Go therefore and make disciples of all nations, baptizing them in the name of the Father and of the Son and of the Holy Spirit, teaching them to observe all that I have commanded you" (Matt. 28:19-20). Jesus orders His first followers to convert the nations to His teaching, and it is through Baptism that this is to happen. In response, Christianity spreads in a manner unheard of in Judaism, eventually converting the entire Roman Empire.

Underlying this missionary zeal is recognition that the acceptance of Christianity has a life-changing impact on the convert. When you look more closely at what drove the Church's missionaries, you find that their guiding light is a strong belief that outside the Church there is no salvation.

How saints and missionaries treat non-Catholic religions demonstrates this implicit and early acceptance of EENS. St. Benedict, the founder of Western monasticism, does not hesitate to destroy the pagan idols of his time:

> The man of God [Benedict] coming to that place broke the idol, overthrew the altar, burned the groves, and of the temple of Apollo made a chapel of St. Martin. Where the profane altar had stood he built a chapel of St. John; and by continual preaching he converted many of the people thereabout.[13]

St. Boniface, the great apostle of Germany, cuts down a pagan sacred tree, called the "Tree of Thor," which the pagans of the area devoutly venerated. Many of the pagans expected him to be killed on the spot by their gods, and when he wasn't, they asked for Baptism.

It was the priority of Baptism (and thus, membership in the Church) that also drove the early Jesuit missionaries. St. Francis Xavier, one of the original Jesuits, baptized thousands of people in Asia in the first half of the sixteenth century. St. Isaac Jogues,

---

[13] Pope Pius XII, *Fulgens Radiatur*, 11.

a missionary to North America a century later, endured incred-ible hardships, including torture. But he felt these hardships were worthwhile:

> God makes himself felt with an abundance of consola-tion. He protects us among the barbarians with so much love. He consoles us with such great tenderness in the little afflictions that we have to endure, that there is not the slightest regret over that which we have given up for him. Nothing can equal, or even approach, the satisfac-tion that our hearts feel in revealing the knowledge of the true God to these infidels. We have baptized about two hundred and forty of them this year. Among these are some whom I have washed in the waters of baptism, and who are assuredly in Paradise, since some of them were small babies of one or two years of age.[14]

In the first half of the twentieth century, the importance of missionary work was stressed by several popes. Writing in 1919, Pope Benedict XV notes:

> According to a recent estimate, the number of non-believers in the world approximates one billion souls. The misfortune of this vast number of souls is for Us a source of great sorrow. From the days when We first took up the responsibilities of this apostolic office We have yearned to share with them the divine blessings of the Redemption.[15]

---

[14] Letter of St. Isaac Jogues to his mother, June 5, 1637, quoted in Francis Talbot, *Saint Among Savages* (San Francisco: Ignatius Press, 2002), 104-105.

[15] Pope Benedict XV, *Maximum Illud*, 6-7.

Pope Benedict XV calls all Catholics to support missionaries by prayer, fostering vocations, and financial support. He says such support is necessary to help souls be rescued from the "domination of Satan":

> Does not the law of charity bind even more strictly when there is even more at stake than the rescue of enormous numbers of people from hunger and destitution and the other forms of physical suffering? Does not this law bind us more stringently when the issue is also, and primarily, the rescue of this stupendous multitude of souls from the arrogant domination of Satan, and their entrance into the freedom of the children of God?[16]

Just a few years later, in 1926, Pope Pius XI returns to the subject of the importance of missionary work in his encyclical *Rerum Ecclesiae*. Early on, he establishes the reason for this work:

> We [have] determined to leave nothing undone which might, by means of apostolic preachers, extend farther and farther the light of the Gospel and make easy for heathen nations the way unto salvation.[17]

And twenty-five years later, Pope Pius XII also emphasizes Catholic missions. In his 1951 encyclical *Evangelii Praecones*, he notes that there are more than 26,000 priests involved in the missions throughout the world, stating, "The object of missionary activity, as all know, is to bring the light of the Gospel to new races and to form new Christians."[18]

---

[16] Pope Benedict XV, *Maximum Illud*, 36.
[17] Pope Pius XI, *Rerum Ecclesiae*, 3.
[18] Pope Pius XII, *Evangelii Praecones*, 22.

For all these popes, it is the belief that the Church is necessary for salvation that drove them to encourage the missions. For Catholic missionaries, and for the popes who supported them, the purpose of the missions was the salvation of souls, which they believed was only possible through the waters of Baptism. This, in turn, was the assumption of the average Catholic too: Baptism—and thus membership in the Catholic Church—was necessary for salvation.

This attitude is the logical conclusion of firm acceptance of the dogma of *extra Ecclesiam nulla salus*. Catholics in 1940 or 1840 or 1340 or 340 would agree: one must be Catholic to be saved, and so we need to do what we can to bring non-Catholics to the Church.

Set Apart

Paradoxically, while the doctrine of EENS spurred the Church to missionary activity, it also led most Catholics to avoid close contact with non-Catholics. Generally speaking, Catholics were urged to avoid close relationships with non-Catholics; non-Catholics were to be converted, not befriended. They were seen as "schismatics," "heretics," or "pagans," to be avoided since they could lead Catholics astray.

The language used by Church leaders over the centuries makes clear the separation between Catholics and non-Catholics. In 1756, Pope Benedict XIV writes an encyclical to Eastern Catholic bishops (those bishops who celebrate the rites of the East but are in union with Rome). In it, he uses only one word to describe the Orthodox: "schismatic." Early in the document he writes, "We have made every attempt to induce the schismatics to abandon their errors and join Us in Catholic unity."[19] Benedict XIV is

---

[19] Pope Benedict XIV, *Ex Quo*, 1.

simply employing the long-standing language of the Church, a practice that persists into the twentieth century. Even as late as 1923, this language is used. In that year, Pope Pius XI writes an encyclical on St. Josaphat, a man who was born into an Orthodox family but later converted to Catholicism. Pius XI writes that Josaphat was "born of schismatic parents";[20] not "Orthodox" parents, but "schismatic" parents.

Additionally, the Church's outlook toward non-Catholics went beyond mere language. Catholics were urged to avoid any close interaction with non-Catholics. In 1832, Pope Gregory XVI writes an encyclical on "mixed marriages," i.e., marriages between Catholics and non-Catholics. "The Apostolic See [Rome] has always ensured that the canons forbidding the marriages of Catholics with heretics have been observed religiously," he writes. "Occasionally such marriages have been tolerated in order to avoid more serious scandals. But, even then, the Roman Pontiffs saw to it that the faithful were taught how deformed these marriages are and what spiritual dangers they present."[21] One of the dangers of such marriages, according to Gregory XVI, is that "some of these misguided people attempt to persuade themselves and others that men are not saved only in the Catholic religion, but that even heretics may attain eternal life."[22] In other words, the doctrine of EENS is what drives Gregory XVI to condemn mixed marriages. This discipline regarding marriage makes clear to the average Catholic that non-Catholic religions are not equal to Catholicism, and that they are dangers to be avoided as much as possible.

[20] Pope Pius XI, *Ecclesiam Dei*, 9.
[21] Pope Gregory XVI, *Summo Iugiter Studio*, 1.
[22] Pope Gregory XVI, *Summo Iugiter Studio*, 2.

In the early twentieth century, the "ecumenical" movement begins within Protestantism. The hope expressed by its leaders is the reunification of all Christians, who have been divided for so long. However, Catholic leaders do not embrace this movement, for they believe true Christian unity comes only by way of all Christians becoming Catholic. Further, they suspect that involvement in the ecumenical movement will lead Catholics to become more like Protestants than the other way around. In 1919, the Catholic Church is invited to participate in a Protestant ecumenical "Faith and Order" conference. Pope Benedict XV refuses to take part. He then has the Holy Office issue a decree prohibiting all Catholics from taking part in conferences dealing with Christian unity being held by non-Catholics, unless permission is explicitly given by the Vatican.

This policy continues under the next pope, Pius XI. Writing in 1928, he says that "it is clear that the Apostolic See [Rome] cannot on any terms take part in their [Protestant ecumenical] assemblies, nor is it anyway lawful for Catholics either to support or to work for such enterprises; for if they do so they will be giving countenance to a false Christianity, quite alien to the one Church of Christ."[23] Here again we see EENS as the driving force in the Church's ecumenical and interreligious outlook.

Even as late as 1959, on the eve of the Second Vatican Council, popes consider their primary duty regarding non-Catholics to be calling them to join the Catholic Church. In that year, Pope John XXIII writes the encyclical *Ad Petri Cathedram*, in which he directs the following words to non-Catholic Christians: "It is the will of God, the Church's founder, that all the sheep should eventually gather into this one fold [the Catholic

---

[23] Pope Pius XI, *Mortalium Animos*, 8.

Church], under the guidance of one shepherd. All God's children are summoned to their father's only home, and its cornerstone is Peter."[24] Further, in the prayers said during the pre-Vatican II Good Friday liturgy, the Church explicitly prays "for heretics and schismatics: that our Lord God would rescue them from all their errors; and recall them to their holy Mother, the Catholic and Apostolic Church."[25]

The attitude Rome takes toward other religions over the centuries filters down to the diocesan level and to the laity. A few examples, taken from the Cincinnati-based *Catholic Telegraph* in 1920 and 1921, should suffice to illustrate.

The November 4, 1920, issue of the *Catholic Telegraph* runs the headline, "Prague Heretics Seek to Obtain Possession of the Church of the Blessed Virgin."[26] The article is about an attempt by a non-Catholic church in Czechoslovakia to take over a Catholic church, with the paper boldly declaring those non-Catholics to be "heretics."

Later in that same issue is an article about the state of the Church in Germany after World War I. It condemns those who had left the Church during that turbulent time under the sub-heading "Apostasy of Weaklings."[27]

Perhaps the most telling example is found in the recommended activities for Catholics during the Church Unity Octave in the January 13, 1921, issue. One recommendation is that the laity should, "Resolve to watch, work and pray every day and at all times for the conversion of your non-Catholic neighbors."[28] The

[24] Pope John XXIII, *Ad Petri Cathedram*, 68.
[25] Good Friday liturgy, 1962 Missal.
[26] *Catholic Telegraph* 89, no. 45, November 4, 1920, 2.
[27] *Catholic Telegraph* 89, no. 45, November 4, 1920, 3.
[28] *Catholic Telegraph* 90, no. 2, January 13, 1921, 4.

idea of "dialoguing" with non-Catholics is unheard of; the duty of the Catholic is to convert them.

Clearly the Church's ecumenical and interreligious outlook has historically been two-fold: (1) Catholics should avoid close relationships with non-Catholics, who were on the path to eternal damnation; and (2) any personal interaction that does occur should be directed toward working for the conversion of the non-Catholics. Before the 1960s, this is the attitude that permeates the Church, from the pope to the lowliest layman.

4

Can a Non-Catholic Be Saved?

From this brief review, the Church's historical ecumenical and interreligious outlook should now be plain. If you are Catholic, you need to stay Catholic, and if you are not Catholic, you need to become Catholic. Clear-cut, right? For the average Catholic, it was. He assumed non-Catholics were on a path to Hell and so either avoided them (to safeguard his own salvation) or tried to convert them (so that they might attain salvation). The idea that other religions were equal to Catholicism or could save souls was unthinkable.

Extraordinary Means

That being said, remember when I noted earlier that a common reaction today to the phrase "outside the Church there is no salvation," is "But what about ... "? Now we will address that question. Although it's always been true that the Church teaches that outside her there is no salvation, it's also true that over time the Church begins to recognize some *extraordinary means* of salvation. These extraordinary means represent a developed understanding of Church doctrine, particularly when it comes to Baptism. The ordinary means (water Baptism) address what *we* must do; the extraordinary means address what *God* can do — how

He can work outside water Baptism. Throughout Church history, speculation about these extraordinary means has been mostly the purview of theologians and the hierarchy. However, we'll see that starting in the 1960s some of these extraordinary means begin to take center stage instead of sitting on the peripheries of the Church as they had for centuries before.

Early in the Church's history there were those who were killed for Christ but had not received water Baptism. These courageous martyrs who gave their entire life for Christ were considered to have undergone a "Baptism of blood," enabling them to enter Heaven immediately. St. Bede, writing in the eighth century, tells the story of a pagan executioner who was converted during the martyrdom of St. Alban, which likely occurred in the early fourth century. This executioner was then also beheaded. St. Bede writes of this unbaptized man, "though he was not purified by the waters of baptism, yet he was cleansed by the washing of his own blood, and rendered worthy to enter the kingdom of heaven."[29] Bede's belief was not controversial in the early Church, which recognized the ultimate sacrifice the martyr offers. Of course, such situations happened only rarely (most Christian martyrs were already baptized at the time of their deaths).

A "Baptism of blood" was not the only non-water, non-sacramental Baptism the Church considered, however. Another type of Baptism, which would become far more controversial, is what is called "Baptism by desire" — the belief that someone who *desires* Baptism can in some sense be considered already baptized. The Church's greatest theologian, St. Thomas Aquinas, writes in the thirteenth century:

---

[29] St. Venerable Bede, *Ecclesiastical History*, 1.7.

The sacrament of Baptism may be wanting to anyone in reality but not in desire: for instance, when a man wishes to be baptized, but by some ill-chance he is forestalled by death before receiving Baptism. And such a man can obtain salvation without being actually baptized, on account of his desire for Baptism, which desire is the outcome of "faith that worketh by charity," whereby God, Whose power is not tied to visible sacraments, sanctifies man inwardly.[30]

So how about the atheist who decides to convert to Catholicism but gets killed in a car accident on his way to his Baptism at the Easter Vigil? What happens to his soul? Is he damned to Hell because he wasn't baptized (and wasn't martyred)? Does his desire to be baptized count for anything? The Church has traditionally recognized that, yes, the catechumen's explicit desire for Baptism was sufficient for salvation.

That example seems pretty clear-cut. However, the acceptance of membership in the Church by someone who simply *desires* Baptism has provided the opportunity for more broad speculations about the salvation of members of other religions. St. Thomas himself notes the possibility of an "implicit" Baptism of desire:

A person receives the forgiveness of sins before baptism in so far as he has baptism of desire, *explicitly or implicitly*; and yet when he actually receives baptism, he receives a fuller remission, for the remission of the entire punishment.[31]

---

[30] St. Thomas Aquinas, *Summa Theologica* III, q. 68, art. 2.

[31] Aquinas, *Summa Theologica* III, q. 69, art. 2, ad. 2, emphasis added.

In the time of St. Thomas, an implicit Baptism of desire was mostly theoretical. Catholics of the time believed that the Gospel had been preached throughout the world, and so anyone who was not Christian had explicitly rejected the Faith and was therefore damned. However, with the discovery of the New World, these assumptions were shattered.

Ignorance Is an Excuse?

Starting in the sixteenth century, Catholic theologians debated the status of those peoples in the New World who had died without hearing of Christianity. Were they damned? Or could they have been saved, much like Jews and Gentiles before the time of Christ were eligible for salvation? Perhaps they implicitly desired Baptism and would have chosen it if they had known about it.

This thinking led to the development of the idea of "invincible ignorance." The foundation for invincible ignorance, like many Catholic theological concepts, can be found in the writings of St. Thomas Aquinas. When discussing ignorance and whether it is a sin, he writes:

> Wherefore through negligence, ignorance of what one is bound to know, is a sin; whereas it is not imputed as a sin to man, if he fails to know what he is unable to know. Consequently ignorance of such like things is called "invincible," because it cannot be overcome by study. For this reason such like ignorance, not being voluntary, since it is not in our power to be rid of it, is not a sin: wherefore it is evident that no invincible ignorance is a sin.[32]

---

[32] Aquinas, *Summa Theologica* I-II, q. 76, art. 2.

While not directly addressing the issue of the salvation of non-Catholics, he does note that invincible ignorance — being unaware of something through no fault of one's own — is not sinful.

This thirteenth century notion did not immediately lead to widespread acceptance by Catholics that those who were truly ignorant of the Gospel could be saved. No — the great missionaries, including those to the New World, were driven by the thought that pagan peoples were damned to Hell. The sixteenth century Spanish Dominican theologian Francisco de Vitoria did not think invincible ignorance was a convincing argument that the inhabitants of the New World were saved:

> When we postulate invincible ignorance on the subject of baptism or of the Christian faith, it does not follow that a person can be saved without baptism or the Christian faith. For the aborigines to whom no preaching of the faith or Christian religion has come will be damned for mortal sins or for idolatry, but not for the sin of unbelief.[33]

Yet the idea begins to develop among Catholic theologians that perhaps salvation would be possible to someone who, through no fault of his own, was ignorant of Jesus Christ. Another Spanish Dominican, Domingo Soto, who was writing at the time of the Council of Trent (1545-1563), concluded that if Gentiles before Christ could have an implicit faith in him, then so could those in the New World.[34] This eventually became the established position of many Catholic theologians.

---

[33] Francisco de Vitoria, *De Indis et de Iure Belli Relectiones*, quoted in Sullivan, *Salvation Outside the Church?*, 70.

[34] Sullivan, *Salvation Outside the Church?*, 78.

In the nineteenth century the idea of "invincible ignorance" gained papal approval. In the 1854 allocution *Singulari Quadam*, Pope Pius IX states,

> For, it must be held by faith that outside the Apostolic Roman Church, no one can be saved; that this is the only ark of salvation; that he who shall not have entered therein will perish in the flood; but, on the other hand, *it is necessary to hold for certain that they who labor in ignorance of the true religion, if this ignorance is invincible, are not stained by any guilt in this matter in the eyes of God.*[35]

Pius IX returns to this theme in 1863:

> We all know that those who are afflicted with invincible ignorance with regard to our holy religion, if they carefully keep the precepts of the natural law that have been written by God in the hearts of all men, if they are prepared to obey God, and if they lead a virtuous and dutiful life, can attain eternal life by the power of divine light and grace.[36]

Pius IX teaches that for one who is invincibly ignorant of the Gospel—meaning, through no fault of his own, he knows nothing of Jesus and his teachings—salvation is still possible. This, as the pope said, assumes the person follows the natural law and leads a virtuous life. In a way, this combines the speculations of the theologians Vitoria and Soto: it affirms both Vitoria's assertion that the ignorant are condemned for their immorality, not their ignorance, and Soto's belief that the ignorant can potentially be saved.

---

[35] Pope Pius IX, Allocution *Singulari Quadam* (December 9, 1854), emphasis added.
[36] Pope Pius IX, *Quanto conficiamur moerorei*, 7.

Most Catholic theologians and Church leaders, however, assumed that obtaining salvation while being invincibly ignorant of the Gospel was exceedingly rare. After all, Pope Pius IX notes that this could only happen if one "carefully [kept] the precepts of the natural law" and led a "virtuous and dutiful life." Further, in his 1864 *Syllabus of Errors*, Pius IX condemns the following error: "Good hope at least is to be entertained of the eternal salvation of all those who are not at all in the true Church of Christ."[37]

Simply put, although it is *possible* for a non-Catholic to be saved, Catholics are discouraged from believing it is *probable* that non-Catholics will be saved. Living a virtuous and dutiful life and keeping the precepts of the natural law is incredibly difficult for a Catholic who has access to the sacraments; how much more so for the pagan who does not! Catholics should not presume the salvation of non-Catholics, since in most cases the possibility is considered remote.

The Case of Fr. Feeney

Even acknowledging the chance of extraordinary means of salvation, especially the idea that one can be saved by a Baptism of implicit desire, remained controversial in spite of Pope Pius IX's explanation. In the middle of the twentieth century, this controversy erupted in the public eye with the case of Fr. Leonard Feeney. Fr. Feeney was a Jesuit priest based in the Boston area in the 1940s. Taking the doctrine of *extra Ecclesiam nulla salus* completely literally, he began to preach that water Baptism was absolutely necessary for salvation; that in no case whatsoever could someone be saved who did not receive water Baptism at some point before death. Thus, he not only rejected the idea

[37] Pope Pius IX, *Syllabus of Errors* (1864), 17.

that someone with invincible ignorance could implicitly desire Baptism and be saved, but he also rejected that a person could be saved by a Baptism of blood.

Naturally, Fr. Feeney received pushback from Church authorities. His superiors disciplined him many times, and eventually his case went to the Vatican. The 1949 response by the Holy Office (what is now called the "Congregation for the Doctrine of the Faith") is worth quoting at length. It lays out clearly the Church's official position regarding salvation:

> In his infinite mercy, God willed that, since [the Church] was a matter of the means of salvation ordained for man's ultimate end, not by intrinsic necessity, but only by divine institution, its salutary effects could also be obtained in certain circumstances when these means are only objects of "desire" or of "hope." This point was clearly established at the Council of Trent, with regard to both the sacrament of Baptism and of penance (Denzinger, n. 797 and 807).
>
> The same must be said of the Church, as a general means of salvation. That is why for a person to obtain his salvation, it is not always required that he be de facto incorporated into the Church as a member, but he must at least be united to the Church through desire or hope.
>
> However, it is not always necessary that this hope be explicit as in the case of catechumens. When one is in a state of invincible ignorance, God accepts an implicit desire, thus called because it is implicit in the soul's good disposition, whereby it desires to conform its will to the will of God.[38]

---

[38] Letter *Suprema haec sacra.*

So on the eve of the 1960s, the Church settles authoritatively that there is at least the *possibility* of salvation for non-Catholics, as long as they are united with the Church through desire.

Summary: The Catholic View of
Other Religions before the 1960s

Before the 1960s, the average Catholic understood the Catholic Church as the unique means of salvation. A person, in most cases, had to receive water Baptism in order to be saved. Further, even the baptized Catholic had to continue to receive the sacraments and remain in good standing with the Church. If he did that, he would one day go to Heaven.

The *Baltimore Catechism*, which was first published in the late nineteenth century and was the standard catechetical text for American Catholic children in the mid-twentieth century, provides an illustration:

166. *Are all obliged to belong to the Catholic Church in order to be saved?*

All are obliged to belong to the Catholic Church in order to be saved.

167. *What do we mean when we say, "Outside the Church there is no salvation?"*

When we say, "Outside the Church there is no salvation," we mean that Christ made the Catholic Church a necessary means of salvation and commanded all to enter it, so that a person must be connected with the Church in some way to be saved.[39]

---

[39] Kelley, *Baltimore Catechism*, No. 2.

While the phrase "in some way" suggests the extraordinary means of salvation, look at the primary emphasis of Question 167:

- Christ set up the Church for the salvation of souls.
- He commands all to enter it.
- To be saved, we must be connected to the Church.

It was reasonable not to emphasize the extraordinary means when most of the world had been exposed to the Gospel or was being evangelized by Catholic missionaries. The martyrdom of unbaptized believers certainly wasn't common, and Baptism by desire was seen as a rare occurrence. Extraordinary means, then, were truly extra-ordinary.

Because of this worldview, Catholics who were not missionaries knew they were to be careful in their interactions with non-Catholics. Associating too closely with non-Catholics could put one's own eternal destination at risk. The infamous Catholic "ghettos" in America and Britain in the nineteenth and early twentieth century might have developed due to discrimination and other outside forces, but they were ultimately *self-imposed* ghettos. Interaction with the outside world was to be directed toward its conversion, not its acceptance. If Catholics had any interaction with non-Catholics, it was much like what Derek Worlock, Archbishop of Liverpool (1976-1996), recounts:

> I was brought up not to enter a Protestant building, let alone take an active part in what took place there. Even to be present at the funeral or wedding of a non-Catholic relation required ecclesiastical permission and due care not to give the impression of taking part in the recitation of Protestant prayers or in hymn singing.[40]

[40] Quoted in Stephen Bullivant, *Mass Exodus* (Oxford: Oxford University Press, 2019), 98-99.

Such restrictive practices—which today appear harshly judgmental—were normal for Catholics of the time. These policies assumed that Catholics were different, or, more accurately, that their religion was different from all others. It was *unique*, and the consequences of this uniqueness impacted their lives both here on earth as well as in Heaven. Catholics lived differently than non-Catholics here, and, as a consequence, Catholics would likely be the only ones who would end up in Heaven.

A 1960 Catholic would likely sum up the Church's teaching as: be baptized and live as a Catholic and you can go to Heaven; don't be Catholic and almost certainly go to Hell. Theologians might nitpick over the extraordinary means of salvation, but the pew-sitting Catholic assumed those extraordinary means were few and far between. In the next section, however, we'll find that in the 1960s those extraordinary means begin to move to center stage, leading to a revolution in how Catholics view—and interact with—other religions. This revolution, in turn, radically alters the fundamental beliefs of Catholics worldwide, and leads to the catastrophic loss of the Church's mission.

II. The Emphasis Shift

Social revolution swept the world, particularly the Western world, in the 1960s. Almost everything that was held sacred was questioned, and beliefs and practices that were previously considered taboo were now pushed toward the mainstream. The same was true within the Catholic Church. In a short period of time, fundamental teachings of the Church came into question, and the beliefs of many Catholics were recast. Many truths considered inviolate by Catholics in 1960 were doubted by those same Catholics in 1970.

This questioning and doubt impacted every aspect of Church life, including the Church's conception of her role in salvation, as well as the role of other religions. Whereas before Catholics were sure of the necessity of the Catholic Church for salvation, now many proposed the Catholic Church as just one viable option among many religions. Fewer Catholics worried about the salvation of their non-Catholic friends and family members. Far fewer were driven to participate in or support the missions. And most tragically, many became indifferent to religion, leading a large number to leave their own practice of the Catholic Faith.

So how did this happen?

Many factors contributed to these changes, but it was an Emphasis Shift within the Church that primarily led to this widespread religious indifference. It was not a direct change in Church teaching. Rather, Church leaders from popes to parish priests shifted how they presented the role of the Church as well as the role of other religions in the process of salvation. Instead of emphasizing the ordinary means of salvation, they put the extraordinary means front-and-center through their statements, actions, and inactions. By doing so, they altered the foundational beliefs of millions of Catholics across the globe.

5

Making a Shift

One of the guiding principles of Catholic belief is *Lex orandi, lex credendi*, "the law of what is to be prayed [is] the law of what is to be believed." This means that how Catholics pray, especially their liturgical prayer, represents what they believe and also that what they believe is represented in how they pray.

With this in mind, consider the following three prayers from the Good Friday liturgy of the late 1950s:

Let us pray ... for heretics and schismatics: that our Lord God would rescue them from all their errors; and recall them to their holy Mother, the Catholic and Apostolic Church.

Let us pray ... for the Jews: that almighty God may remove the veil from their hearts; so that they too may acknowledge Jesus Christ our Lord.

Let us pray ... for pagans: that almighty God would remove iniquity from their hearts: that, putting aside their idols, they may be converted to true and living God and His only Son, Jesus Christ our God and Lord.

These prayers represent well what Catholics had been taught for centuries and what they believed as the 1960s approached. Non-Catholics were seen as different from Catholics and in need of conversion. To the average Catholic of the time, the prayers would not be controversial — the law of prayer is the law of belief.

Now compare those prayers to the corresponding prayers found in the Good Friday liturgy promulgated in 1970, just a decade later:

> Let us pray ... for all our brothers and sisters who believe in Christ, that our God and Lord may be pleased, as they live in truth, to gather them together and keep them in his one Church.

> Let us pray ... for the Jewish people, to whom the Lord our God spoke first, that he may grant them to advance in love of his name and in faithfulness to his covenant.

> Let us pray ... for those who do not believe in Christ, that, enlightened by the Holy Spirit, they, too, many enter the way of salvation.

In these prayers, it's unclear what the Church actually desires God to do. In the case of non-Catholic Christians (who went from "heretics and schismatics" to "our brothers and sisters who believe in Christ"), it appears they are already "in his one Church," so they just need to stay there. The prayer for the Jewish people doesn't seem to ask them to change their religion, and the prayer for "those who do not believe in Christ" (referred to previously as "pagans") just ambiguously asks for their salvation without noting if Christianity has any role in that process. Even if it's possible to squint hard and claim that the prayers have the same basic intentions as before, the overall outlook of the Church toward other religions is fundamentally altered.

The Origin of the Changes

Any observer of twentieth-century Catholicism recognizes that there are significant differences in how the religion was practiced before the 1960s as compared with after the 1960s. We see it clearly in the Good Friday prayers I noted above, and we could give endless other examples: the Mass, parish life, acceptance of moral teachings, and on the list could go.

The radical changes have inspired a host of theories as to why this happened.

The quasi-official line we hear from most Church leaders is that the Church needed to change how she did things to better address the modern world. St. Paul declared, "I have become all things to all men, that I might by all means save some" (1 Cor. 9:22), and proponents of the Emphasis Shift argue that this is what the Church did: she adapted to modern times in order to reach more people with the Gospel.

However, some Catholics argue that the Church simply gave way to the prevailing culture, allowing herself to become too much like the world, violating another of St. Paul's declarations, "Do not be conformed to this world but be transformed by the renewal of your mind" (Rom. 12:2). The abandonment of Catholicism by millions of priests, nuns, and lay people following the 1960s — along with the Church's declining influence on society and culture — are proof enough that the Church's shift went too far. Even if Church leaders had good intentions in making the changes, the results have been disastrous. (Some Catholics might feel uncomfortable with critiques of popes, bishops, and other Church leaders. If this is the case for you, please see Appendix A, "Can Catholics Criticize Popes and Councils?")

Still others have argued that these weren't simply good intentions gone awry, but that the Church was infiltrated by subversive elements. Enemies of the Church obtained high-ranking and influential positions within the Church in order to corrupt her. They shifted the emphasis in a direct, planned attempt to change Catholics' beliefs.

In this book, I am not diving into the underlying "why" of the Church's changes; I'm looking at the actions that instigated the changes and the consequences of those changes. Whether the changes were intentional or accidental, what matters most is their dramatic impact on the world's largest and one of its oldest religions. If you showed the average 1950s Catholic a snapshot of Catholicism in 2020 with no explanation, he would likely think it was a different religion. Yet many 1950s Catholics did in fact accept the shift in the Church as it was introduced (although many left the Church as well). This is due to how these changes came about.

How Catholics Come to Their Beliefs

So what was the method that caused these widespread changes to occur? Church leaders manifested a significant Emphasis Shift, not a radical change in official teaching, particularly when it came to how the Church perceived herself and how she perceived the value of other religions. This Emphasis Shift retained previous official Church teaching but nevertheless led to a change in the beliefs of millions of Catholics worldwide.

This touches on the topic of how Catholics come to their beliefs in the first place. Many of us have a caricatured view of this: the pope or an ecumenical council teaches something,

Catholics believe it. Yet reality is much more nuanced than that. Catholics have countless "teachers" that help form their beliefs, and those "teachers" include a pastor's homilies, media reports, Church documents, home life, papal interviews, peer influence, and many other sources. Also, what is *not* said may be as important as what is said.

For example, consider Catholics' opinions about artificial contraception. The official teaching of the Church, which has been reiterated many times by popes (most famously in 1968 in Pope Paul VI's encyclical *Humanae Vitae*) is that the use of artificial contraception is always immoral. Yet surveys have repeatedly shown that the vast majority of Catholics today see nothing wrong with contraception. How did so many Catholics come to a conclusion so at odds with the official teaching?

An easy answer would be to simply say that Catholics let the surrounding culture teach them. Artificial contraception is widely accepted in today's world, and in fact the few who hold differing views are ridiculed as "outdated" or even "regressive." It's true that the culture has been a significant teacher of Catholics when it comes to contraception.

Yet it's also true that the actions — and inactions — of both clerics and laypeople in the Church have "taught" that artificial contraception is in fact okay to use. Throughout the first half of the twentieth century everyone knew that the Catholic Church taught that artificial contraception was immoral. This was clear and well-known. But this began to change in the 1960s. In some cases, priests (and even bishops) publicly preached that the use of artificial contraception is moral, or they downplayed the teaching, apparently embarrassed by it. In other cases, priests told penitents in the confessional that it's not a sin they need to confess. Theologians found ways to diminish or deny the immorality of contraception, or they treated it as an antiquated issue that should be ignored. Most commonly, contraception has simply not been discussed from the pulpit or anywhere else in the parish, creating the impression that the Church looks on contraception no differently than the wider world or that its differing perspective is something to subscribe to only if one happens to agree. Even when bishops or priests hold to the Church's teaching regarding contraception, in most cases they shift their emphasis to downplay its immorality.

This has led to a vast breach between magisterial Church teaching—which never changed—and how Catholics have actually been taught. It would be easy to see all these other "teachers" as unofficial and therefore not important, but that would ignore the very real way the Catholic Faith has always been passed on from generation to generation since the time of Christ. The Church is not a "document Church," simply consisting of declarations and teachings to which we must assent. It is a living Body made up of men and women that passes on the Faith in all the ways humans have always passed on knowledge. So even though the Church officially teaches that the use of artificial contraception is immoral, from the perspective of the average Catholic, "the Church" appears at least ambivalent toward its use, and perhaps even supportive of the practice. The shift in emphasis regarding contraception led to a massive change in beliefs, even when magisterial teaching didn't change.

This is an important point, so I want to make it as clear as possible. Imagine the following scenario. A father of a young son is a big New York Yankees fan. He watches as many Yankee games as he can, he wears a Yankees hat all the time, and he has Yankees posters in his house. By the time his son is six years old, he's also rooting hard for the Yankees. But then, Dad starts watching fewer Yankees games. He stops wearing his Yankees hat, and he takes down the posters. When asked, he will tell his son he's still a Yankees fan, although he doesn't root for them anymore. Then one day, when his son is ten, the father puts a Boston Red Sox poster up in the house and starts watching more and more Red Sox games, but he still insists to his son that he's a Yankees fan. By the time his son is fifteen, the father rarely talks about the Yankees, but he does discuss the ins and outs of Red Sox baseball. Yet still, if his son asks, he admits he is a Yankees fan.

When the son grows up and leaves the house, do you think he'll be a Yankees fan? Perhaps, but it wouldn't be surprising if he ended up a Red Sox fan or started rooting for another team or even stopped being a baseball fan altogether. His father never explicitly rejected Yankees fandom, and in fact continued to claim it over the years, but he *shifted his emphasis* to the Red Sox. This shift sent confusing signals to his son, and, at least implicitly, it told him that he no longer thought the Yankees were the team to root for.

This analogy shows how *a shift in emphasis by someone in authority, while verbally maintaining the same "official" position, can lead to a change in belief in those under his authority*. That, I believe, is what happened starting in the 1960s in the Catholic Church. Church leaders adopted an Emphasis Shift, while retaining the Church's official teachings. This Emphasis Shift filtered down to all the various "teachers" of the faith that influence Catholic belief.

A Three-Fold Emphasis Shift

The last chapter recounted the established conviction of the Church and Catholics worldwide in the 1950s: it is necessary to be Catholic in order to be saved, although in very rare cases perhaps a non-Catholic could make it to Heaven. Yet we know that this isn't the majority view among Catholics today; a recent Pew Study showed that 68 percent of Catholics believe non-Catholic religions can lead to eternal life.[41] Even though the Church did not change her official core teachings, the Emphasis Shift that started in the 1960s led to a change of beliefs by millions of Catholics worldwide.

This Emphasis Shift consisted of three aspects. *First*, the Church changed her focus from proclaiming the Gospel to non-Catholics to desiring "dialogue" with them. *Second*, the Church toned down her proclamations of Catholicism as the sole path to Heaven. And *third*, the Church no longer warned against the errors of non-Catholic religions, instead highlighting the beliefs held in common with Catholicism.

This three-fold Emphasis Shift, whether executed with good or with nefarious intentions, has had far-reaching consequences in the life of the Church; it has led to widespread religious indifference among Catholics, which in turn has smothered the Church's zeal for souls. That's why it's so important to understand how it happened.

---

[41] Pew Research Center, "U.S. Public Becoming Less Religious," November 3, 2015, https://www.pewforum.org/2015/11/03/chapter-1-importance-of-religion-and-religious-beliefs/#paths-to-eternal-life.

6

From Proclamation to Dialogue

After Pope John XXIII announced in 1959 that he would convene an ecumenical council, the Vatican took more than two years to prepare for it to commence. A primary task was the preparation of *schemata*, which were intended to be draft versions of documents that the Council fathers would use to produce the official Council texts. However, very soon after the Council convened, these *schemata* were set aside and it was decided that new drafts would be prepared from scratch. Although the documents were discarded, they represent a final glimpse at the Church's ecumenical and interreligious outlook before the Emphasis Shift took firm hold.

One aspect of this pre-Shift outlook was the priority of conversion, including the conversion of non-Catholic Christians. In the *schema* of the Dogmatic Constitution on the Church, one passage addresses how Catholics should engage with individual non-Catholic Christians:

> The Catholic Church, knowing that separated Christians are deprived of many of the means of salvation and that by their separation the manifestation of the unity of the sign lifted up among the nations is in fact obscured, looks

with maternal love upon them individually and lovingly invites them to herself. Therefore, this Holy Synod approves the initiatives of Catholics by which separated brethren are being enlightened about the teaching and life of the Church so that even individually they may be drawn towards her, and it urges that such efforts be still further promoted.[42]

The substance of this passage is on bringing non-Catholic Christians into formal membership in the Church. (Although note the use of the term "separated brethren" instead of "heretics" and "schismatics" when referring to Protestants and Orthodox Christians—already there is a subtle shift in the language even in these preparatory *schemata*.)

The draft document then addresses how the Church should approach entire non-Catholic Christian communities, stating,

While not denying that the elements retained by these communities can be salvific there also and can produce the fruits of a Christian spiritual life, this Sacred Synod nevertheless firmly teaches that the fullness of revelation was entrusted by Christ solely to the Catholic Church, that it cannot be divided, and that, therefore, it is there that it must be acknowledged by all Christians. Therefore, this holy Synod admonishes all the faithful more and more by word and example to show the separated brethren that the fullness of revelation is truly and purely maintained only in the Catholic Church, and to do this in such a way that when finally our brothers are again

[42] Preparatory Theological Commission, *De Ecclesia*, chap. 11, unpublished trans. by Fr. Joseph Komonchak.

linked with us, they may with us also possess the fullness of Christ's heritage.[43]

Before Vatican II began, the Church's ecumenical outlook, at least as presented in this *schema*, is two-fold: emphasize that only in the Catholic Church can be found the "fullness of revelation," and urge Catholics to engage in the *proclamation* of the Gospel to non-Catholics for the purpose of their conversion. However, within a few short years of drafting this *schema*, a new word replaces "proclamation" as the centerpiece of interreligious activity. That word is "dialogue," and the person who brings that term to the forefront is Pope Paul VI.

Introducing Dialogue

Giovanni Cardinal Montini is elected pope on June 21, 1963, after the death of Pope John XXIII. The Second Vatican Council has already held one session in late 1962, and there is some question whether the new pope will continue the Council or disband it. He quickly indicates that he wants Vatican II to go on. Before his election, Montini was known as a moderately "progressive" bishop, and as Archbishop of Milan he encouraged more extensive ecumenical relations with non-Catholic religions. Many observers both then and today consider Paul VI's papacy as simply a continuation of the papacy of Pope John XXIII's, but it is under Paul VI, not John XXIII, that we witness the dramatic Emphasis Shift that alters the course of the Church in significant ways.

In August 1964, between the second and third sessions of Vatican II, Paul VI releases his first encyclical, *Ecclesiam Suam*. Often a pope's first encyclical sets the theme for his pontificate,

---

[43] Preparatory Theological Commission, *De Ecclesia*, chap. 11.

and this is particularly true of *Ecclesiam Suam* and Paul VI. Early on in the letter the pope signals the methodology of the Emphasis Shift: "This encyclical intends neither to claim a solemn and strictly doctrinal function, nor to propose particular moral or social teachings, but merely to communicate a fraternal and informal message."[44] New doctrines will not be explicitly declared, but how existing doctrines are presented will change. Instead of defining doctrine or setting disciplines as popes in the past have done, Paul VI sets a deliberately conversational, non-confrontational tone, a tone in keeping with the theme of this encyclical: "dialogue."

The term "dialogue" is common today within the Church, but at the time of *Ecclesiam Suam* it was not. No previous papal encyclical or council document in the history of the Church uses the term in the way Paul VI does, including the two Vatican II documents that were already released by that time — *Sacrosanctum Concilium* (The Constitution on the Sacred Liturgy) and *Inter Mirifica* (The Decree on the Means of Social Communication). Yet after the release of Paul VI's *Ecclesiam Suam*, "dialogue" becomes one of the most important and most influential terms in the Catholic Church. *Ecclesiam Suam* fundamentally altered how the Church interacts with non-Catholics.

Section III of *Ecclesiam Suam* is simply titled "The Dialogue." In this section, Paul VI lays out his vision for a Church interacting with the world. He begins by stating, "There is [an] attitude which the Catholic Church should adopt at this period in the history of the world, an attitude characterized by study of the contacts which the Church ought to maintain with humanity."[45]

---

44 Pope Paul VI, *Ecclesiam Suam*, 7.
45 Pope Paul VI, *Ecclesiam Suam*, 58.

He continues by explaining the "distinction" between the Church and the world. But then the pope states, "this distinction is not a separation."[46] This is the initiation of the Emphasis Shift. In the past, the Church considered herself a separate society; in the world, but not of it. The work of evangelization and missions was to bring pagans and other non-Catholics into the fold. Paul VI does not deny that mission, but he begins the process of emphasizing the commonality between the world and the Church, rather than its separateness.

The pope introduces the means by which the Church and the world should interact: "The Church should enter into dialogue with the world in which it exists and labors."[47] Strangely, he then recasts the work of his papal predecessors as the work of dialogue:

> Nor can we do otherwise in our conviction that the dialogue ought to characterize our Apostolic Office, heirs as we are of such a pastoral approach and method as has been handed down to us by our predecessors of the past century, beginning with the great, wise Leo XIII. Almost as a personification of the Gospel character of the wise scribe, who, like the father of a family, "knows how to bring both new and old things out of his treasure-house," in a stately manner he assumed his function as teacher of the world by making the object of his richest instruction the problems of our time considered in the light of the Word of Christ.
>
> Thus, also, did his successors, as you well know.
>
> Did not our predecessors, especially Pope Pius XI and Pope Pius XII, leave us a magnificently rich patrimony

46 Pope Paul VI, *Ecclesiam Suam*, 63.
47 Pope Paul VI, *Ecclesiam Suam*, 65.

of teaching which was conceived in the loving and enlightened attempt to join divine to human wisdom, not considered in the abstract, but rather expressed in the concrete language of modern man? *And what is this apostolic endeavor if not a dialogue?*[48]

Later in the encyclical Paul VI declares dialogue a divine mandate: "Deeply engraved on our heart are those words of Christ which we would humbly but resolutely make our own: 'When God sent His Son into the world, it was not to reject the world, but so that the world might find salvation through Him.' See, then, Venerable Brethren, *the transcendent origin of the dialogue. It is found in the very plan of God.*"[49] Dialogue, according to Paul VI, is how God relates to mankind, and therefore should be how the Church relates to the world.

Yet historically *proclamation*, not conversation, has been how the Church interacts with the world. The Church proclaims the Gospel, and then the Holy Spirit works in the hearts of those who hear the proclamation to convert them. The model of proclamation-which-leads-to-conversion is found at the very foundations of the Church, all the way back to the first Christian (and papal) sermon, given by St. Peter at Pentecost (Acts 2:14-36). Our first pope declares to the crowd that Jesus Christ is the fulfillment of Old Testament promises and that Christ is the one who brings salvation to all. When the crowd then asks Peter what they should do, he responds, "Repent, and be baptized every one of you in the name of Jesus Christ for the forgiveness of your sins; and you shall receive the gift of the Holy Spirit" (Acts

[48] Pope Paul VI, *Ecclesiam Suam*, 67-68, emphasis added.
[49] Pope Paul VI, *Ecclesiam Suam*, 69-70, emphasis added.

2:38). There is no discussion or dialogue between the parties: Peter *proclaims* the Gospel, and then the people, by the power of the Holy Spirit, convert.

Yet in *Ecclesiam Suam*, proclamation takes a back seat to dialogue. Instead of regarding the world in need of conversion to Christ, it is primarily considered something to work with for the betterment of mankind on earth. The impact of the Church's dramatic Emphasis Shift represented by *Ecclesiam Suam* cannot be overestimated. This shift upends the entire paradigm in how the Church relates to the world, a paradigm that had existed for more than 1,900 years, and replaces it with a novel, unproven method of engaging the outside world.

Impacting the Council

The shift that results during Vatican II reveals the immediate impact of *Ecclesiam Suam*. Neither of the Council documents produced before *Ecclesiam Suam* mentions dialogue, but the term is peppered throughout the documents that come after it. We find it employed particularly in the three documents that are addressed to the outside world: *Unitatis Redintegratio* (Decree on Ecumenism), *Ad Gentes* (Decree on the Church's Missionary Activity), and *Gaudium et Spes* (Pastoral Constitution on the Church in the Modern World).

Actually, the original draft of *Unitatis Redintegratio* does not even include the word "dialogue," but the revised version, which was presented after the release of *Ecclesiam Suam*, puts the term front and center. In regard to how the Church should relate to both non-Catholic Christians and the wider world, dialogue is now the key that unlocks the Church's understanding of her outward mission. In addition, the very existence of a formal "Decree on Ecumenism" is itself a major shift in emphasis. Whereas popes before

John XXIII condemned involvement in the ecumenical movement and called for the return of wayward "schismatics" (Eastern Orthodox Christians) and "heretics" (Protestant Christians), here is a Council document encouraging the ecumenical movement and calling for "dialogue" with non-Catholic Christians.

Unitatis Redintegratio begins by laying out the Catholic principles for ecumenism, stating,

> The term "ecumenical movement" indicates the initiatives and activities planned and undertaken, according to the various needs of the Church and as opportunities offer, to promote Christian unity. These are: first, every effort to avoid expressions, judgments and actions which do not represent the condition of our separated brethren with truth and fairness and so make mutual relations with them more difficult; then, "dialogue" between competent experts from different Churches and Communities. At these meetings, which are organized in a religious spirit, each explains the teaching of his Communion in greater depth and brings out clearly its distinctive features. In such dialogue, everyone gains a truer knowledge and more just appreciation of the teaching and religious life of both Communions.[50]

Unitatis Redintegratio defines here the purpose of dialogue: to explain one's teachings to others, and to listen to their explanations so that each party gains better knowledge and "appreciation" of the other. Note what is *not* the purpose of dialogue: conversion. In fact, conversion isn't once mentioned in *Unitatis Redintegratio*, other than to note that all Christians desire "one visible Church of God, a Church truly universal and set forth

[50]   *Unitatis Redintegratio*, 4.

into the world that the world may be converted to the Gospel and so be saved, to the glory of God."[51] There is no particular call for non-Catholic Christians to convert to Catholicism or for Catholics to seek their conversion.

Ecumenism, by its very nature, downplays the need for non-Catholics to convert. This attitude permeates Vatican II. In fact, *every* document is influenced by ecumenical sensibilities, not just *Unitatis Redintegratio*. As I'll detail later, a Secretariat for Promoting Christian Unity was formed before the Council began, and its duty was to make sure all the Council texts were considered in the light of ecumenism, as Bishop Emile De Smedt of Belgium noted on the Council floor.[52] Contrast this to the words of Pope Pius IX before Vatican I a century earlier. He invited "all Protestants and other non-Catholics" to use the occasion of Vatican I "to return to the Catholic Church."[53] The Emphasis Shift could not be more clear: dialogue with non-Catholic Christians, not a call to return to the Catholic Church, is now the order of the day.

The call to dialogue is not limited to the Eastern Orthodox and Protestants; it extends to pagans and other non-Christians. In *Ad Gentes*, the Decree on the Church's Missionary Activity, the Council fathers write of the training needed for missionary priests: "priestly training should have an eye to the pastoral needs of that region; and the students should learn the history, aim, and method of the Church's missionary activity, and the special social, economic, and cultural conditions of their own people. Let them be educated in the ecumenical spirit, and duly *prepared for*

---

[51] *Unitatis Redintegratio*, 1.

[52] Ralph Wiltgen, S.V.D., *The Inside Story of Vatican II* (Charlotte, NC: TAN Books, 2014), 61.

[53] Wiltgen, *The Inside Story of Vatican II*, 172.

fraternal dialogue with non-Christians."[54] The document also notes the role of laymen in missionary works: "Worthy of special praise are those laymen who, in universities or in scientific institutes, promote by their historical and scientific religious research the knowledge of peoples and of religions; thus helping the heralds of the Gospel, and *preparing for the dialogue with non-Christians.*"[55] Dialogue with non-Christians — rather than a proclamation that seeks their conversion — moves to center stage in the Church's missionary work.

Finally, the Council also calls for dialogue with "the world." *Gaudium et Spes*, the Pastoral Constitution on the Church in the Modern World, is the final document promulgated by the Council, and it is intended as the capstone crowning the Catholic Church's new attitude toward the world. No longer are condemnation or separation to be the watchwords between Church and world; now, *Gaudium et Spes* declares the new watchword will be *dialogue*:

> By virtue of her mission to shed on the whole world the radiance of the Gospel message, and to unify under one Spirit all men of whatever nation, race or culture, the Church stands forth as a sign of that brotherhood which allows honest dialogue and gives it vigor ... the desire for such dialogue, which can lead to truth through love alone, excludes no one, though an appropriate measure of prudence must undoubtedly be exercised. We include those who cultivate outstanding qualities of the human spirit, but do not yet acknowledge the Source of these qualities. We include those who oppress the Church and

[54] *Ad Gentes*, 16, emphasis added.
[55] *Ad Gentes*, 41, emphasis added.

harass her in manifold ways. Since God the Father is the origin and purpose of all men, we are all called to be brothers. Therefore, if we have been summoned to the same destiny, human and divine, we can and we should work together without violence and deceit in order to build up the world in genuine peace.[56]

In the Gospel of John, the "world" is repeatedly set in contrast to Jesus and his followers. It is something to be converted, not emulated or even "understood," to use modern terminology. Jesus is seen as the divine Judge of the World: "And this is the judgment, that the light has come into the world, and men loved darkness rather than light, because their deeds were evil" (John 3:19). "Now is the judgment of this world, now shall the ruler of this world be cast out" (John 12:31). Yet in *Gaudium et Spes* the world is something that works together with the Church; an entity not in opposition to the Church, but a partner. Specifically, a partner in dialogue.

To be clear, the explosion of the use of the term "dialogue" by the Church, while a radical departure from how the Church operated in the past, is not a change in official Church teaching. Rather, it's a clear shift in practical emphasis. Catholics are now called not to separate themselves from non-Catholics, or work to convert them, but instead to engage in dialogue with them, explaining Catholicism, but also learning and appreciating what non-Catholics, both Christian and non-Christian, believe. We'll find later that, as benign as it might sound, this aspect of the Emphasis Shift has major ramifications on the beliefs of the average Catholic.

---

[56] *Gaudium et Spes*, 92.

7

From Unique to One among Many

Downplaying the uniqueness of Catholicism is the second aspect of the three-fold Emphasis Shift that occurs during the 1960s. As detailed previously, it is a fundamental teaching of Catholicism that "outside the Church there is no salvation" (*extra Ecclesiam nulla salus*). In other words, the Catholic Church is the *unique* means by which we are saved. Historically, this teaching was interpreted rather strictly: Catholics believed that, with a few exceptions, one has to be a visible member of the Church (via Baptism) in order to be saved. However, the foundations of this bedrock belief begin to crumble in short order in the 1960s, again through a *shift in emphasis*.

"Subsists in"

The most visible and infamous example of this Emphasis Shift is found in the Vatican II document, *Lumen Gentium* (Dogmatic Constitution of the Church). Intending to answer the question, "What is the Church?" the document states in article 8:

> Christ, the one Mediator, established and continually sustains here on earth His holy Church, the commu-nity of faith, hope and charity, as an entity with visible

delineation through which He communicated truth and grace to all ... This is the one Church of Christ which in the Creed is professed as one, holy, catholic and apostolic, which our Saviour, after His Resurrection, commissioned Peter to shepherd, and him and the other apostles to extend and direct with authority, which He erected for all ages as "the pillar and mainstay of the truth." *This Church constituted and organized in the world as a society, subsists in the Catholic Church*, which is governed by the successor of Peter and by the Bishops in communion with him, although many elements of sanctification and of truth are found outside of its visible structure. These elements, as gifts belonging to the Church of Christ, are forces impelling toward catholic unity.[57]

The phrase "subsists in the Catholic Church" was at the time—and still is—incredibly controversial. Why not just say that Christ's Church "is" (Latin: *est*) the Catholic Church? After all, that is the term commonly used in Church documents for centuries before Vatican II. In 1943, Pope Pius XII wrote that the "true Church of Jesus Christ ... is the One, Holy, Catholic, Apostolic and Roman Church."[58] The *Baltimore Catechism* (which was written almost 100 years before Vatican II) used the word "is" to reflect the relationship between Christ's Church and the Catholic Church:

152. *Which is the one true Church established by Christ?*
     The one true Church established by Christ is the Catholic Church.[59]

---

[57] *Lumen Gentium*, 8, emphasis added.
[58] Pope Pius XII, *Mystici Corporis*, 13.
[59] Kelley, *Baltimore Catechism*, no. 2.

Why then does the Council instead say "subsists in" (Latin: *subsistit in*)? Some claim that "subsists in" and "is" have the same meaning; others regard "subsists in" as an explicit acknowledgement that Christ's Church exists outside the visible boundaries of the Catholic Church as well as within her.

Adding to the controversy, the original draft of this Dogmatic Constitution on the Church is much more direct in its language. It states,

> The holy Synod teaches and solemnly professes, therefore, that there is only a single true Church of Jesus Christ, that Church which in the Creed we proclaim to be one, holy, catholic and apostolic, the Church which the Savior acquired for himself on the cross and joined to himself as body to head and as bride to bridegroom, the Church which, after his resurrection, he handed over to be governed to St. Peter and his successors, the Roman Pontiffs. Therefore, only the Catholic Roman is rightly called the Church.[60]

Yet the final approved text abandons this strong language and uses the phrase "subsists in" to describe the relationship between the Church of Jesus Christ and the Catholic Church. Gregory Baum, an Augustinian priest and influential theological advisor at Vatican II, writes shortly after *Lumen Gentium*'s promulgation that he believes the change in language reflects a change in teaching:

[60] Preparatory Theological Commission, *De Ecclesia*, chap. 1; cf. Michael Davies, *Pope John's Council* (Kansas City: Angelus Press, 2007), 90.

Instead of simply identifying
the Catholic Church, the Cons
carefully that the Church of Christ
lic Church. The body of Christ is pre
Church, but, at the same time, without l
and incarnate nature, *transcends* it.[61]

The language used by *Lumen Gentium* leads   to agree
with Baum, with some even going so far as to say that the Catholic Church no longer held herself to be the one true Church. In
the fifteenth edition of the *Encyclopaedia Britannica* (published in
1974), the entry for "Roman Catholicism" states, "The Roman
Catholic Church has officially abandoned its 'one true church'
position." This entry was written by a Catholic priest, Fr. John
L. McKenzie, S.J.[62]

However, almost forty years after the release of *Lumen Gentium*, the Congregation for the Doctrine of the Faith (led at the
time by Cardinal Joseph Ratzinger, the future Pope Benedict
XVI) declares that such an interpretation is incorrect:

> The interpretation of those who would derive from the
> formula *subsistit in* the thesis that the one Church of
> Christ could subsist also in non-Catholic Churches and
> ecclesial communities is therefore contrary to the au-
> thentic meaning of *Lumen gentium*. The Council instead
> chose the word *subsistit* precisely to clarify that there exists
> only one "subsistence" of the true Church, while outside
> her visible structure there only exist *elementa Ecclesiae*,

---

[61] Quoted in Davies, *Pope John's Council*, 90 (emphasis added).
[62] Quoted in H. J. A. Sire, *Phoenix from the Ashes* (Brooklyn: Angelico Press, 2015), 382.

which — being elements of that same Church — tend and lead toward the Catholic Church.[63]

Yet, as we have seen, a change in official teaching is not necessary to make a dramatic impact in what Catholics believe; a shift in emphasis is a powerful force. Many Church leaders, theologians, and lay people interpret the shift to the phrase "subsists in" as a clear sign that Catholics should de-emphasize the unique nature of the Catholic Church.

Anonymous Christians

Related to the debate regarding the relationship between the Catholic Church and Christ's Church, yet perhaps more influential on the average Catholic, is the rise of the concept of the "Anonymous Christian." This idea is made popular by the German Catholic theologian and Jesuit priest Karl Rahner in the early 1960s. He describes it thus:

> "Anonymous Christianity" means that a person lives in the grace of God and attains salvation outside of explicitly constituted Christianity. A Protestant Christian is, of course, "no anonymous Christian"; that is perfectly clear. But, let us say, a Buddhist monk (or anyone else I might suppose) who, because he follows his conscience, attains salvation and lives in the grace of God; of him I must say that he is an anonymous Christian; if not, I would have to presuppose that there is a genuine path to salvation that really attains that goal, but that simply has nothing to do with Jesus Christ. But I cannot do that. And so if I hold if

---

[63] Congregation for the Doctrine of the Faith, *Dominus Iesus* (August 6, 2000), footnote 56.

everyone depends upon Jesus Christ for salvation, and if at the same time I hold that many live in the world who have not expressly recognized Jesus Christ, then there remains in my opinion nothing else but to take up this postulate of an anonymous Christianity.[64]

Rahner is trying to balance two competing beliefs: first, that Jesus Christ is the only way to salvation; and second, that people can be saved without explicitly acknowledging Jesus as Lord. Although throughout Church history the emphasis has always been on the former while the latter possibility was seen as at best an extremely rare and extraordinary exception, Rahner puts it front and center in his theology of the Anonymous Christian.

Rahner is no obscure theologian, formulating idiosyncratic beliefs in an academic setting. He is one of the most influential Catholic theologians of the twentieth century, and he exercises a heavy influence on Vatican II. Pope John XXIII himself appointed Rahner as a *peritus* (theological advisor) to the Council, and Rahner is one of seven theologians chosen to develop *Lumen Gentium*. In that document we find hints of Rahner's theory of the Anonymous Christian, particularly in paragraph 16.

First, let's consider the context. In paragraph 14, *Lumen Gentium* describes those who are full members of the Catholic Church:

They are fully incorporated in the society of the Church who, possessing the Spirit of Christ accept her entire system and all the means of salvation given to her, and

---

[64] Karl Rahner, Paul Imhof, and Hubert Biallowons, *Karl Rahner in Dialogue: Conversations and Interviews, 1965-1982* (New York: Crossroad, 1986), 135.

are united with her as part of her visible bodily structure and through her with Christ, who rules her through the Supreme Pontiff and the bishops.[65]

Then *Lumen Gentium* recognizes the unique place in the Church for catechumens:

Catechumens who, moved by the Holy Spirit, seek with explicit intention to be incorporated into the Church are by that very intention joined with her. With love and solicitude Mother Church already embraces them as her own.[66]

As we know, this is traditional Catholic teaching: baptized members of the Church, as well as catechumens desiring Baptism, are part of the Church and thus able to obtain salvation.

In paragraph 15, *Lumen Gentium* addresses non-Catholic Christians (i.e., Orthodox and Protestants) and expresses a desire for full Christian unity. Finally, in paragraph 16, the subject of non-Christians is raised. First, the Jewish people:

In the first place we must recall the people to whom the testament and the promises were given and from whom Christ was born according to the flesh. On account of their fathers this people remains most dear to God, for God does not repent of the gifts He makes nor of the calls He issues.[67]

No explicit mention is made of whether Jews can be saved if they remain Jews, and there is likewise no call to convert them.

[65] *Lumen Gentium*, 14.
[66] *Lumen Gentium*, 14.
[67] *Lumen Gentium*, 16.

Next, *Lumen Gentium* moves to those who "acknowledge the Creator," particularly Muslims:

> But the plan of salvation also includes those who acknowledge the Creator. In the first place amongst these there are the Muslims, who, professing to hold the faith of Abraham, along with us adore the one and merciful God, who on the last day will judge mankind.[68]

The ambiguous language used here raises many questions: How does the plan of salvation include them? How is it that Muslims adore God "with us" when they reject who God is — the Blessed Trinity? And again there is no call to convert Muslims or others who "acknowledge the Creator."

Then we get to the section in which Rahner's "Anonymous Christian" theory appears to be explicitly endorsed:

> Nor is God far distant from those who in shadows and images seek the unknown God, for it is He who gives to all men life and breath and all things, and as Saviour wills that all men be saved. *Those also can attain to salvation who through no fault of their own do not know the Gospel of Christ or His Church, yet sincerely seek God and moved by grace strive by their deeds to do His will as it is known to them through the dictates of conscience.* Nor does Divine Providence deny the helps necessary for salvation to those who, without blame on their part, have not yet arrived at an explicit knowledge of God and with His grace strive to live a good life.[69]

---

[68] *Lumen Gentium*, 16.
[69] *Lumen Gentium*, 16, emphasis added.

This passage patently affirms that someone who is not Catholic, or even Christian, can "attain to salvation." In addition, the wording that they "also" can attain salvation implies that those mentioned before—Orthodox, Protestants, Jews, Muslims, monotheists—are all also able to "attain to salvation." If, then, this is true, what is the purpose of the Catholic Church?

It's hard to find a more clear-cut case of the Emphasis Shift in how Catholics regard the necessity of the Church for salvation. Whereas before the doctrine that "outside the Church there is no salvation" was clearly proclaimed, now those outside the visible boundaries of the Church are solemnly declared able to "attain to salvation." The extraordinary means of salvation are stretched and opened to accommodate anyone and everyone, no matter their religious background. Although *Lumen Gentium* leaves ambiguous *how* non-Catholics are saved, this document, with its dependence upon the theory of the Anonymous Christian, and its shift in emphasis from previous Church pronouncements, is the cornerstone for the now-widespread belief among Catholics that other religions can lead a person to eternal life.

Religious Liberty

Another way in which the Church shifted her emphasis to downplay her uniqueness is by her embrace of the concept of religious liberty in the Vatican II document *Dignitatis Humanae*, the Declaration on Religious Liberty. Many commentators consider *Dignitatis Humanae* to be the most controversial of all the Council documents.

Traditionally, the Catholic Church saw a tight interweaving between the Church and the State. This is particularly the fruit of medieval Christendom, in which the State supported and advanced the work of the Church, and the Church helped direct the policies of the State. Of course, in the modern West, and especially in America, this stance has been relegated to an eccentric belief (and perhaps even a dangerous idea). Yet even in the early twentieth century it was still a common belief both among Church leaders and lay Catholics. While it was acknowledged that in pluralistic nations like the United States, various religions would need to be tolerated, the ideal was still the "Catholic State," which would work together with the Church for the common good.

Writing in 1906, Pope Pius X notes,

> That the State must be separated from the Church is a thesis absolutely false, a most pernicious error. Based, as it is, on the principle that the State must not recognize any religious cult, it is in the first place guilty of a great injustice to God; for the Creator of man is also the Founder of human societies, and preserves their existence as He preserves our own.[70]

A result of this union between Church and State is the fact that the Catholic religion should be preferred and given rights that other religions do not possess, because it is only the Catholic religion that is true. Error, according to the Church, has no rights. Those who follow other religions while living in a Catholic State, therefore, do not have complete and total liberty to practice those religions. In Catholic thought, restrictions placed on the practitioners of other religions are based on the conviction that the practice of the proper religion is paramount and of more import than the secular concerns of the State. As Pius X notes, "But as the present order of things is temporary and subordinated

---

[70] Pope Pius X, *Vehementer Nos*, 3.

to the conquest of man's supreme and absolute welfare, it follows that the civil power must not only place no obstacle in the way of this conquest, but *must aid us in effecting it.*"[71]

Such an attitude had an obvious impact on how Catholics regard other religions. American Catholics might have to accept the Pluralism of the country as a reality, but even then the ultimate goal is to have a Catholic State that favors the One True Church and restricts the practice of other religions.

Dignitatis Humanae, however, marks a significant change in how the Church perceives the role of the State when it comes to other religions. Now the Church explicitly advocates that all men have a right to worship as they wish:

> This Vatican Council declares that the human person has a right to religious freedom. This freedom means that all men are to be immune from coercion on the part of individuals or of social groups and of any human power, in such wise that no one is to be forced to act in a manner contrary to his own beliefs, whether privately or publicly, whether alone or in association with others, within due limits.
>
> The council further declares that the right to religious freedom has its foundation in the very dignity of the human person as this dignity is known through the revealed word of God and by reason itself. *This right of the human person to religious freedom is to be recognized in the constitutional law whereby society is governed and thus it is to become a civil right.*[72]

---

[71] Pope Pius X, *Vehementer Nos*, 3, emphasis added.
[72] *Dignitatis Humanae*, 2, emphasis added.

Whereas before the Church advocated that the Catholic religion deserved civil rights that other religions did not, now she is saying that all religions share in those rights.

It is not the point of this book to debate the merits or demerits of religious freedom. Most Catholics today cherish religious freedom and in fact rightly fear that modern efforts to restrict it will likely damage, not advance, the cause of the Church. But it's important to note that this aspect of the Emphasis Shift impacts the way Catholics judge other religions. Before, the Church was put on a pedestal: she did not engage in ecumenical discussions with non-Catholic Christians, and she deserved rights that other religions did not deserve. She was different, unique, set apart. Now, however, the Church herself is saying that she should be considered on the same playing field as other religions, both in ecumenical and interreligious dialogue as well as in regard to the civil authorities. This Emphasis Shift naturally changes the perception of Catholics: instead of considering their Church the One True Religion, they perceive her simply as One Option Among Many.

8

From Warning against Errors
to Promoting Commonalities

The third aspect of the threefold Emphasis Shift in the 1960s Church is the move from warning against the errors of non-Catholic religions to promoting what they hold in common with Catholicism. Historically, the Church considered those outside her confines as schismatics, heretics, or pagans, all in need of conversion to the One True Religion of Catholicism. However, beginning in the early 1960s, the emphasis moves to finding points of unity with non-Catholics and noting only the positive aspects of non-Catholic religions.

Before we explore this aspect of the Emphasis Shift, it's important to understand the Catholic conception of the religious world. Imagine a circle with a small ring in the center and consecutively larger rings moving outwards like the age rings that are visible in the cross-section of a tree. The Catholic Church is in the center, and then non-Catholic religious groups are designated by their closeness to Catholicism, from the Eastern Orthodox (very close) all the way to atheists (far away).

Further, the Catholic Church more broadly breaks the non-Catholic religious world into two main categories: non-Catholic

Christians (including Orthodox churches and Protestant Communities), and non-Christian religions (including Judaism, Islam, and all other religions). In official Church parlance, relations with non-Catholic Christians are called "ecumenism" and relations with non-Christian religions are called "interreligious dialogue."

In 1960, the Vatican begins to build structures for formal relations with these two categories of peoples. First, on June 5, 1960, Pope John XXIII establishes the Secretariat for Promoting Christian Unity (later renamed the Pontifical Council for Promoting Christian Unity). This Secretariat is charged with participating in the ecumenical movement (relations with non-Catholic Christians). The very existence of this Secretariat represents a major Emphasis Shift by Rome. Previous popes had discouraged and at times even forbidden Catholic involvement in the ecumenical movement. Now the pope is creating a formal Vatican structure to do what was previously forbidden!

A few years later, in 1964, Pope Paul VI establishes the Secretariat for Non-Christians (later renamed the Pontifical Council for Interreligious Dialogue). Similar to the Secretariat for Promoting Christian Unity, this Vatican structure is to give attention to relations with those who are not Christian—Jews, Muslims, and other non-Christians. In previous ages, the main attention Rome gave non-Christians was missionary work for their conversion, but now the emphasis is shifted toward official dialogue (a dialogue, as we'll later see, that never includes proclamation of the Gospel).

In addition to the formation of these two secretariats, Church leaders make ecumenical and interreligious outreach one of the most important themes of the Council. The Secretariat for Promoting Christian Unity not only helps draft the document on ecumenism, it also helps the Council fathers evaluate *all* Council documents from the point of view of ecumenism. Ecumenism becomes a primary lens through which all Catholic doctrine and practice is to be interpreted.

Vatican II also formally addresses the Church's relations with other religions in two separate documents:

- *Unitatis Redintegratio* — The Decree on Ecumenism
- *Nostra Aetate* — The Declaration on the Relation of the Church to Non-Christian Religions

We've already learned that *Unitatis Redintegratio* emphasizes dialogue over conversion. In addition, these two documents set the tone for the Church's reimagined relations with non-Catholics, moving from an era of warning against non-Catholic errors to promoting what non-Catholics share in common with Catholics.

Ecumenism

Before the 1960s, we know that the Catholic Church discouraged or even forbade participation in the ecumenical movement. Church leaders interpreted this movement as an attempt to unite Christians under something other than the true Church of Christ, the Catholic Church. The emphasis of the Catholic Church was rather to call non-Catholic Christians to return to the one fold. As Pope Leo XIII wrote in 1894 of Protestants, "Suffer that We should invite you to the unity which has ever existed in the Catholic Church and can never fail; suffer that We should lovingly hold out Our hand to you. The Church, as the common mother of all, has long been calling you back to her."[73]

With the advent of the papacy of John XXIII in the late 1950s to the early 1960s, however, that all begins to change. The pontiff makes sure that both Orthodox and Protestant leaders are invited

---

[73] Leo XIII, *Praeclara Gratulationis Publicae*.

as non-voting observers at the Council. And in 1961, for the first time, a pope officially gives permission for Catholic participation in an ecumenical World Council of Churches conference, to be held in New Delhi.[74] Very quickly the Church has shifted her emphasis from caution toward and distrust of ecumenical activities to encouraging participation in them. Vatican II, in *Unitatis Redintegratio*, solidifies this Emphasis Shift and makes it official:

> In certain special circumstances, such as the prescribed prayers "for unity," and during ecumenical gatherings, it is allowable, *indeed desirable* that Catholics should join in prayer with their separated brethren. Such prayers in common are certainly an effective means of obtaining the grace of unity, and they are a true expression of the ties which still bind Catholics to their separated brethren.[75]

Beyond calling for dialogue with non-Catholics, another shift in emphasis found in the Vatican II documents including *Unitatis Redintegratio* is the portrayal of other religions. Whereas historically the Church noted the deficiencies in other religions, she now seems concerned only with what is shared in common. For comparison look at just one example from the late-nineteenth-century Pope Leo XII:

> We now look upon the nations who, at a more recent date, were separated from the Roman Church by an extraordinary revolution of things and circumstances. Let them forget the various events of times gone by, let

---

[74] Cited in Robert McAfee Brown, *The Ecumenical Revolution: An Interpretation of Catholic-Protestant Dialogue* (Garden City, NJ: Doubleday & Company, 1967), 54.

[75] *Unitatis Redintegratio*, 8, emphasis added.

them raise their thoughts far above all that is human, and seeking only truth and salvation, reflect within their hearts upon the Church as it was constituted by Christ. If they will but compare that Church with their own communions, and consider what the actual state of Religion is in these, they will easily acknowledge that, forgetful of their early history, *they have drifted away, on many and important points, into the novelty of various errors*; nor will they deny that of what may be called the Patrimony of Truth, which the authors of those innovations carried away with them in their desertion, there now scarcely remains to them any article of belief that is really certain and supported by Authority.[76]

The errors of Protestantism are highlighted, and Protestants are called to return to the Catholic Church. Compare that with the language of *Unitatis Redintegratio*:

In the great upheaval which began in the West toward the end of the Middle Ages, and in later times too, Churches and ecclesial Communities came to be separated from the Apostolic See of Rome. Yet *they have retained a particularly close affinity with the Catholic Church* as a result of the long centuries in which all Christendom lived together in ecclesiastical communion.[77]

Rather than pointing out Protestantism's rejection of vital doctrine, this passage fixates on the extent to which its beliefs align with Catholic beliefs. There is no denial or reversal of

---

[76] Pope Leo XII, *Praeclara Gratulationis*, emphasis added.
[77] *Unitatis Redintegratio*, 19, emphasis added.

previous Catholic doctrine in *Unitatis Redintegratio*, yet there is a significant shift in emphasis.

Interreligious Dialogue

With the promulgation of the document *Nostra Aetate* Vatican II also addresses the Church's relations with non-Christian religions. *Nostra Aetate* is the shortest of the 16 Council documents, and it was originally intended to address only the Church's relations with the Jews; however, it was broadened to include all non-Christians religions, and in particular Islam, Buddhism, and Hinduism.

Unlike statements directed toward non-Catholic Christians separated from Rome, the Church rarely addressed non-Christian religions in an official capacity before *Nostra Aetate*. *Nostra Aetate* is the first Church document to address specifically the Church's relations with Jews. The very existence of *Nostra Aetate*, then, is itself a significant shift in emphasis. And again, like *Unitatis Redintegratio*, it concentrates not on what separates these religions from Catholicism, but what they have in common with the Church. Consider *Nostra Aetate*'s opening words:

> In our time, when day by day mankind is being drawn closer together, and the ties between different peoples are becoming stronger, the Church examines more closely her relationship to non-Christian religions. In her task of promoting unity and love among men, indeed among nations, she considers above all in this declaration what men have in common and what draws them to fellowship.[78]

Of the Jews, *Nostra Aetate* states:

[78] *Nostra Aetate*, 1.

As the sacred synod searches into the mystery of the Church, it remembers the bond that spiritually ties the people of the New Covenant to Abraham's stock. Thus the Church of Christ acknowledges that, according to God's saving design, the beginnings of her faith and her election are found already among the Patriarchs, Moses and the prophets. She professes that all who believe in Christ — Abraham's sons according to faith — are included in the same Patriarch's call, and likewise that the salvation of the Church is mysteriously foreshadowed by the chosen people's exodus from the land of bondage. The Church, therefore, cannot forget that she received the revelation of the Old Testament through the people with whom God in His inexpressible mercy concluded the Ancient Covenant. Nor can she forget that she draws sustenance from the root of that well-cultivated olive tree onto which have been grafted the wild shoots, the Gentiles. Indeed, the Church believes that by His cross Christ, Our Peace, reconciled Jews and Gentiles, making both one in Himself.[79]

Regarding Muslims, *Nostra Aetate* remarks that "the Church regards with esteem also the Moslems,"[80] and urges Catholics to shift the emphasis away from our differences toward working together for the common good:

Since in the course of centuries not a few quarrels and hostilities have arisen between Christians and Moslems, this sacred synod urges all to forget the past and to work

---

[79] *Nostra Aetate*, 4.
[80] *Nostra Aetate*, 3.

sincerely for mutual understanding and to preserve as well as to promote together for the benefit of all mankind social justice and moral welfare, as well as peace and freedom.[81]

Nostra Aetate neatly sums up this aspect of the Emphasis Shift in paragraph 2:

The Catholic Church rejects nothing that is true and holy in these religions. She regards with sincere reverence those ways of conduct and of life, those precepts and teachings which, though differing in many aspects from the ones she holds and sets forth, nonetheless often reflect a ray of that Truth which enlightens all men.... The Church, therefore, exhorts her sons, that through dialogue and collaboration with the followers of other religions, carried out with prudence and love and in witness to the Christian faith and life, they recognize, preserve and promote the good things, spiritual and moral, as well as the socio-cultural values found among these men.[82]

The singular emphasis on the positive aspects of non-Catholic religions has led many observers over the years to accuse *Nostra Aetate* of encouraging religious indifference. An authority no less than Pope Benedict XVI notes in 2012, "[*Nostra Aetate*] speaks of religion solely in a positive way, and it disregards the sick and distorted forms of religion."[83] Bishop Athanasius Schneider, auxiliary bishop of Astana, Kazakhstan and a vocal critic of

---

[81] *Nostra Aetate*, 3.

[82] *Nostra Aetate*, 2.

[83] Reflections of His Holiness Benedict XVI, *L'Osservatore Romano*, October 11, 2012. Quoted in Athanasius Schneider, *Christus*

the Church's interreligious outreach, more recently notes that "relativism is already implicitly there ... when ... [*Nostra Aetate*] praises Hinduism as a religion, saying that 'in Hinduism, men contemplate divine mystery.... They seek freedom through a flight to God with love and trust' (n 2). How can you praise a religion which mainly worships idols?"[84]

By shifting the emphasis to noting only the positive aspects of religions, *Nostra Aetate* led many Catholics to consider all religions — even religions the Church officially has always considered false religions — as paths to God, without officially changing a single doctrine.

The Church's three-fold Emphasis Shift in the 1960s began the process of altering how the Church — and the average Catholic — perceived the outside religious world. To continue and solidify this Shift, a new theological edifice would need to be built. As we'll see in the next section, it would be an edifice that would, intentionally or not, be the foundation for widespread religious indifference.

Vincit: Christ's Triumph Over the Darkness of the Age (Brooklyn: Angelico Press, 2019), 95.

[84] Schneider, *Christus Vincit*, 174.

III. The Theological Aftermath

One of the difficulties in analyzing what happened in the Catholic Church after Vatican II is the byzantine complexity of the changes. Within the Church arose many factions and schools of thought, all competing to be considered the True Interpretation of the Council. Factions whose arguments and beliefs agreed on some topics contradicted one another on others. While two groups argued over their differences, a third group looked on and declared them both wrong. Charges of heresy and disobedience flew between camps. Confusion reigned.

In this section, I explain the various theological schools that developed in the aftermath of Vatican II with regard to Catholic teaching on salvation. These schools range from the Absolutist (only baptized Catholics can be saved) to the Universalist (everyone is saved). An understanding of these schools is vital, for it is my contention that a subtle move along this range by prominent theologians and Church leaders led to an embrace of religious indifference by most Catholics. We must grasp these post–Vatican II theological schools to understand how this happened.

DEADLY INDIFFERENCE

Of course the aftermath of the Emphasis Shift isn't limited to university theology departments and Jesuit retreat centers. Theology impacts ministry, and in Section IV we'll survey how popes, bishops, and priests implemented these theological developments into the life of the Church.

9

The Salvation Spectrum

In the wake of Vatican II, Catholic theologians and leaders grapple with the theological implications of the Emphasis Shift, particularly as it pertains to the role of the Church in the process of salvation: the possibility of salvation for individual non-Catholics, as well as whether other religions can lead souls to salvation. An entire spectrum develops, from — on one extreme — those (very few) who still insist that only baptized Catholics can be saved, to — on the other extreme — those who believe that everyone will one day be saved. I will call this collection of shaded distinctions in belief the "Salvation Spectrum."

In this chapter I will give an overview of the spectrum of views on this topic, and then in the next few chapters, I will go into detail regarding the most significant schools of thought. The Salvation Spectrum can be confusing because it encompasses both theology and attitude. The nuances between the different schools are many, and even within one school there may be vast differences in attitude that lead to vigorous debate. Differences in theology — such as a disagreement on whether water Baptism is necessary for salvation — are easy to see and understand. What's less clear but just as important are differences in attitude, such as how easy or difficult one believes it is for a non-Catholic to reach Heaven.

Generally speaking, one's attitude toward mankind's salvation can range from skeptical to hopeful. Do you believe salvation is something that is difficult to obtain, or is it something that most people, assuming they live a decent life, will eventually reach? Of course, your theology of God will shape your attitude. If you see God primarily as a judge, then you will likely see salvation as hard to reach. But if you see God primarily as an indulgent father, then salvation is rather easy to come by. And of course there is a whole range of attitudes between those extremes.

The reason it's important to take into account attitude as part of the Salvation Spectrum is because attitude is one of the primary drivers of religious indifference. Too often the debate among Catholics today is limited to theology. And of course theology is essential. But it's not the only driving force behind the practical beliefs of Catholics worldwide, whether lay or clerical. Attitude matters too. The more liberal your attitude toward salvation, the more likely you are to be religiously indifferent—in practice at least, even if not in theology. If you believe, for example, that most non-Catholics will go to Heaven, then you will see little reason to try to convert them from their religions. If, on the other hand, you think salvation is only for a small subset of humanity, you are more likely to do all you can to convert your loved ones.

In order to make the Salvation Spectrum more understandable, I've created a chart to lay out the various views:

Broadly speaking, we see five main theological schools in this debate: Absolutist, Exclusivist, Inclusivist, Pluralist, and Universalist.[85]

---

[85] These are my names for the various schools; others have given other names and have also used the names I use in different ways than I do.

Salvation Spectrum

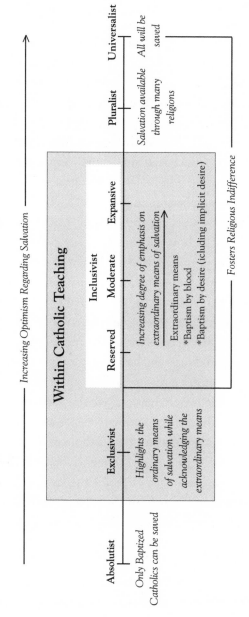

The Salvation Spectrum

The first school, the *Absolutists*, is insignificant in both number and influence today. It includes those who agree with Fr. Feeney (see chapter 4) that only Catholics who have been baptized
by water can be saved. As we have seen, the Church formally
condemned this view in 1949, and now very few hold to it.

The second school, the *Exclusivists*, is also small in number
but has grown in influence in recent years. Prior to the 1960s the
vast majority of Catholics throughout history held this view. The
Exclusivists believe that the Church is necessary for salvation
and emphasize the ordinary means of salvation: water Baptism
and visible membership in the Church. But Exclusivists, unlike
the Absolutists, accept the possibility of extraordinary means
of salvation such as Baptism by desire. However, they do not
presume them nor do they highlight them. As shown in the
Salvation Spectrum, the Exclusivist view is within Catholic
teaching; it conforms to the magisterial teachings of the Church.

The third school, the *Inclusivists*, is the broadest, most diverse
school. The distinctions within the Inclusivist school are mostly
based on attitude and emphasis, not theology. Generally speaking,
Inclusivists accept magisterial Church teaching that "outside the
Church there is no salvation" yet they are salvation optimists.
They highlight the extraordinary means we discussed in chapter
4 and further emphasize what Catholics have in common with
non-Catholics. In terms of influence and number, there is no
question the Inclusivist school is the most predominant. This
is the school of Popes John Paul II and Benedict XVI. Further,
this camp encompasses Catholics across an otherwise diverse
theological and ideological spectrum.

Pluralists comprise the fourth school. These are Catholics
who have embraced the idea that not only can non-Catholics
be saved, but that *they can be saved through the practice of their*

non-Catholic religion. Whereas the end result—salvation optimism for non-Catholics—is similar to the Inclusivist school, the two views are theologically quite different. The Inclusivist insists that a non-Catholic who is saved is still saved through the Church in some mysterious way, but the Pluralist sees other religions as the *means* of a person's salvation. This school, while it has become more prominent since the 1960s, is outside of magisterial Catholic teaching, although we'll see that it has gained more acceptance in recent years from high-ranking members of the Catholic hierarchy.

The fifth and final school goes even further than the Pluralists. The *Universalists* believe that *everyone* will be saved; i.e., Hell (if it even exists) is empty. Within the ranks of Catholic theologians and Church leaders, there are few, if any, who openly advocate this position. Some have publicly said that they *hope* Hell is empty and declare that is a reasonable hope, but most of those who make these statements are theologically members of the Inclusivist school.

Again, much of the debate within Catholic circles since the 1960s has revolved around whether a certain theological view is orthodox or not. While debate like this is important, it fails to completely incorporate how Catholics come to their beliefs. Certain theological schools can remain technically orthodox but still lead Catholics to unorthodox conclusions. For example, the real-world impact of growing salvation optimism among Catholics—whether that attitude is practiced by an Inclusivist or a Universalist—fosters religious indifference all the same. Even though the entire Inclusivist school attempts to maintain orthodox beliefs regarding EENS, the practical implication of highlighting the extraordinary means of salvation is that being Catholic isn't all that important.

10

Salvation Optimism: The Inclusivists

Until the twentieth century, most Catholics were skeptical about the chances of salvation for non-Catholics. This was due to the marked distinction the Church made between the ordinary means of salvation and the extraordinary means. The extraordinary means were truly out of the ordinary, and a Catholic could not presume someone met the conditions necessary for those means. Yet after the Emphasis Shift, Inclusivism came to predominate Catholicism, which pushed the extraordinary means to the forefront, making them in many ways ordinary.

Making the Extraordinary Ordinary

An example of this shift can be seen by comparing the sixteenth-century *Roman Catechism*, which was promulgated in response to the Council of Trent, and the twentieth-century *Catechism of the Catholic Church*, which was a fruit of the Second Vatican Council. Each catechism has a section titled, "The Necessity of Baptism." In the *Roman Catechism*, the first paragraph of this section states plainly,

> If the knowledge of what has been hitherto explained be, as it is, of highest importance to the faithful, it is no

less important to them to learn that the law of Baptism, as established by our Lord, extends to all, so that unless they are regenerated to God through the grace of Baptism, be their parents Christians or infidels, they are born to eternal misery and destruction. Pastors, therefore, should often explain these words of the Gospel: "Unless a man be born again of water and the Holy Spirit, he cannot enter into the kingdom of God" (John 3:5).[86]

Following this paragraph are subsections detailing the necessity of Baptism for both infants and adults. At no point in this section does the *Roman Catechism* mention any of the extraordinary means of salvation.

In the modern *Catechism of the Catholic Church*, however, the extraordinary means of salvation dominate the section titled "The Necessity of Baptism." Even in the first few sentences these means are implied:

> The Lord himself affirms that Baptism is necessary for salvation. He also commands his disciples to proclaim the Gospel to all nations and to baptize them. *Baptism is necessary for salvation for those to whom the Gospel has been proclaimed and who have had the possibility of asking for this sacrament.* (CCC 1257)

Then following this paragraph, the rest of the section details the various extraordinary means. First, it explicitly notes the two extraordinary means (Baptism of blood and the "desire for Baptism" [CCC 1258]). Then the next three paragraphs (CCC

---

86 *Roman Catechism* (Rockford, IL: TAN Books and Publishers, 1982), 176-177.

1259-1261) give examples of how a person could be saved without water Baptism.

This is the heart of Inclusivism: an emphasis on the extraordinary means of salvation, which entirely shifts how one thinks about the importance of the Church in the plan of salvation.

Before the Emphasis Shift most Catholics were skeptical about how often the extraordinary means actually applied to individual souls. This created a missionary fervor to evangelize those who had not heard/received the Gospel, as well as abhorrence of the idea of leaving the Church. However, that skepticism was thrown aside in the 1960s, and today optimism in favor of salvation is widespread among Catholics, including among Catholic theologians and Church leaders. This optimism pervades the attitude of Universalists (obviously) and Pluralists, but it's also the attitude of Inclusivists. The difference is that the Inclusivists, unlike the Universalists and Pluralists, are concerned with reconciling that optimism with official Church teaching. Inclusivists grapple with this simple question: If the Church says it's possible that non-Catholics can be saved (and she does say this), then how easy is it for them to be saved, and by what process are they saved?

First, the question of "how easily?" Generally speaking, whereas before the 1960s Catholics assumed most non-Catholics were not saved, after the Emphasis Shift during that decade Catholics began to assume many, if not most, non-Catholics were saved. Inclusivists embraced this sunny outlook. One primary Biblical passage used to defend this optimism is 1 Timothy 2:3-4, which refers to "God our Savior, who desires all men to be saved and to come to the knowledge of the truth." If the all-powerful God truly desires all men to be saved, doesn't it follow that at least most men are in fact saved? Within the Inclusivist camp there is a range of opinion as to how accessible salvation is to non-Catholics, but all Inclusivists are more hopeful than the average Catholic of, say, a hundred years ago.

The second question — by what process are non-Catholics saved? — leads to complex theological issues. How does one reconcile the outwardly Exclusivist teaching, "outside the Church there is no salvation" with an Inclusivist view that many non-Catholics are in fact saved? Inclusivists have posited many theories, and fierce debate rages within this school as to the details of how God saves non-Catholics.

For purposes of clarity, I have grouped the Inclusivists into three general categories — Reserved, Moderate, and Expansive — which reflects their range of optimism when it comes to the salvation of non-Catholics.

Reserved Inclusivists

One of the best representatives of the Reserved Inclusivist camp is Pope Benedict XVI (formerly Joseph Cardinal Ratzinger). Although he has a reputation in some circles as a strict traditionalist, he more properly falls into the Inclusivist camp when it comes to the issue of salvation. A young priest and official theological consultant to Vatican II in 1964, Ratzinger notes in a sermon,

> Everything we believe about God, and everything we know about man, prevents us from accepting that beyond the limits of the Church there is no more salvation, that up to the time of Christ all men were subject to the fate of eternal damnation. We are no longer ready and able to think that our neighbor, who is a decent and respectable man and in many ways better than we are, should be eternally damned simply because he is not a Catholic. We are no longer ready, no longer willing, to think that

eternal corruption should be inflicted on people in Asia, in Africa, or wherever it may be, merely on account of their not having "Catholic" marked in their passport.[87]

The salvation optimism of this sermon is evident: there seems to be no question for Ratzinger that many non-Catholics can —and *will*—be saved.

Two decades later, Joseph Ratzinger is a Cardinal as well as the head of the Sacred Congregation for the Doctrine of the Faith. His views on the subject of salvation remain the same. In a book-length interview from the mid-1980s called *The Ratzinger Report*, he states, "It is part of the Church's ancient, traditional teaching that every man is called to salvation and de facto can be saved if he sincerely follows the precepts of his own conscience, even without being a visible member of the Catholic Church."[88]

And thirty years later, after his papal retirement, Ratzinger/Benedict still sounds the same notes:

There is no doubt that on this point we are faced with a profound evolution of dogma. While the fathers and theologians of the Middle Ages could still be of the opinion that, essentially, the whole human race had become Catholic and that paganism existed now only on the margins, the discovery of the New World at the beginning of the modern era radically changed perspectives. In the second half of the last century it has been fully affirmed the understanding that God cannot let go to perdition all

---

[87] Joseph Ratzinger, "Are Non-Christians Saved?" https://www.beliefnet.com/faiths/catholic/2007/01/are-non-christians-saved.aspx.

[88] Joseph Cardinal Ratzinger with Vitterio Messori, *The Ratzinger Report* (San Francisco: Ignatius Press, 1985), 196.

the unbaptized and that even a purely natural happiness for them does not represent a real answer to the question of human existence. If it is true that the great missionaries of the 16th century were still convinced that those who are not baptized are forever lost—and this explains their missionary commitment—in the Catholic Church after the Second Vatican Council that conviction was finally abandoned.[89]

This statement represents perhaps the most complete summation of the Church's Emphasis Shift that occurred in the 1960s. In it, the pope recognizes the massive Emphasis Shift, or "evolution of dogma," as he calls it, and he also recognizes that it has had a significant—and negative—impact on the missionary commitment of the Church. Yet he remains a firmly committed Inclusivist, emphasizing that Catholics should no longer believe that "all the unbaptized" will be denied entrance to Heaven.

In spite of this optimistic turn, during his long public life Ratzinger is also one of the clearest Catholic voices insisting that salvation can come only through Christ and the Church. In the same 1964 sermon quoted above, Fr. Ratzinger also says, "A great deal of thought had been devoted in theology, both before and after Ignatius, to the question of how people, without even knowing it, *in some way belonged to the Church and to Christ* and could thus be saved nevertheless."[90] So, for young Fr. Ratzinger, it is obvious that many non-Catholics will be saved,

---

89 "Full Text of Benedict XVI's Recent, Rare, and Lengthy Interview," *Catholic World Report*, March 17, 2016, https://www. catholicworldreport.com/2016/03/17/full-text-of-benedict-xvis -recent-rare-and-lengthy-interview/.

90 Ratzinger, "Are Non-Christians Saved?" emphasis added.

although their salvation will still come through the Church in some mysterious way.

Likewise, in *The Ratzinger Report*, Cardinal Ratzinger emphatically insists that "There is but one savior" and it is Jesus Christ.[91] And in the year 2000, the Congregation for the Doctrine of the Faith, under the direction of Cardinal Ratzinger, releases *Dominus Iesus*, which decisively proclaims that Jesus is the only way to salvation, and that this salvation occurs through Christ's Church (which, it noted, "subsists in" the Catholic Church). We will look more closely at this document in a later chapter.

So how do we reconcile these somewhat confusing statements by Joseph Ratzinger? On the one hand, he freely acknowledges and even emphasizes that non-Catholics can and will be saved. On the other hand, he insists that salvation is only through the Church. This is the crux of the Inclusivist position: to be hopeful about the salvation of non-Catholics while recognizing that salvation still always comes through the Church. *How* that salvation comes to people who are not visible members of the Catholic Church is the debate within the Inclusivist school. For a Reserved Inclusivist like Ratzinger, the role of conscience plays a part, although he completely rejects the "Anonymous Christian" theory pushed by Karl Rahner (an Expansive Inclusivist) or any suggestion that another religion is a means to salvation (the Pluralist position).

Another distinctive feature of Reserved Inclusivists is their sincere concern over the collapse of missionary work in the wake of the Emphasis Shift. In his 1964 sermon, Fr. Ratzinger asks the essential question, "The question that torments us is, much rather, that of why it is still actually necessary for us to carry out

[91] Ratzinger, *The Ratzinger Report*, 196.

the whole ministry of the Christian faith — why, if there are so many other ways to heaven and to salvation, should it still be demanded of us that we bear, day by day, the whole burden of ecclesiastical dogma and ecclesiastical ethics?"[92] He was still asking the question two decades later: "Many a one began to wonder, 'Why should we disturb non-Christians, urging them to accept baptism and faith in Christ, if their religion is *their* way to salvation in their culture, in their part of the world?'"[93] And as recently as 2015, he was *still* asking the question, "Why should one try to convince the people to accept the Christian faith when they can be saved even without it?"[94]

The answer given by Ratzinger, and all Reserved Inclusivists, is ultimately unsatisfying; it is essentially, "Christ told us to evangelize," or "Catholicism is a better way to live than other religions." Concern for the damnation of souls — which was the driving force of Catholic missionaries for almost two millennia — is no longer front and center, for it is no longer considered a likely possibility. Even though Reserved Inclusivists regret the collapse of missionary activity, they are unwilling to return to an outlook that would drive it again.

Moderate Inclusivists

I will not detail the Moderate Inclusivist group extensively because it corresponds closely to the Reserved Inclusivists, albeit with more optimism regarding the salvation of non-Catholics. However, this group does help distinguish the range in attitude that occurs within the broader Inclusivist school.

---

92 Ratzinger, "Are Non-Christians Saved?"
93 Ratzinger, *The Ratzinger Report*, 197.
94 "Benedict XVI's Recent, Rare, and Lengthy Interview."

Pope John Paul II is the primary representative of this group. Like Cardinal Ratzinger (whom John Paul II made head of the Congregation for the Doctrine of Faith), the Polish pope always insisted that salvation comes through Jesus Christ. However, John Paul II's attitude toward non-Catholic Christians was far more accepting than Ratzinger's, and further, he was more inclined toward engaging in interreligious prayer services and praising the values of other religions.

Each man's attitude toward interreligious prayer illustrates the practical difference between John Paul II's outlook and Ratzinger's. Both accepted the legitimacy of the practice, but Ratzinger is far more cautious in his embrace of it than John Paul II. In fact, in John Paul II's first encyclical, *Redemptor Hominis*, he endorses the practice wholeheartedly. After writing of the need for Catholics to work together with non-Catholic Christians, he moves to non-Christians:

> What we have just said must also be applied—although in another way and with the due differences—to activity for coming closer together with the representatives of the non-Christian religions, an activity expressed through dialogue, contacts, *prayer in common*, investigation of the treasures of human spirituality, in which, as we know well, the members of these religions also are not lacking.[95]

Also found in this encyclical is the Moderate Inclusivist praise for other religions, including the belief that the Holy Spirit works within them:

[95] Pope John Paul II, *Redemptor Hominis*, 6, emphasis added.

Does it not sometimes happen that the firm belief of the followers of the non-Christian religions—*a belief that is also an effect of the Spirit of truth operating outside the visible confines of the Mystical Body*—can make Christians ashamed at being often themselves so disposed to doubt concerning the truths revealed by God and proclaimed by the Church and so prone to relax moral principles and open the way to ethical permissiveness?[96]

The caution with which Reserved Inclusivists approach other religions is absent with Moderate Inclusivists like John Paul II. I could give countless examples, but just a few will suffice:

To representatives of the Shinto religion (1979): "I wish to express my respect for the religion you profess. The Catholic Church recognizes with reverence everything that is true, good and noble in your religion."[97]

To a group of Buddhists (1979): "The Catholic Church expresses her esteem for your religion and for your high spiritual values."[98]

To the leaders of various religions in Korea (1984): "I wanted … to express to you my high esteem of the millennia of precious cultural heritage and admirable traditions of which you are the guardians and living witnesses."[99]

---

[96] Pope John Paul II, *Redemptor Hominis*, 6, emphasis added.

[97] Quoted in *Interreligious Dialogue: The Official Teaching of the Catholic Church (1963-1995)* (Boston: Pauline Book & Media, 1997), 215.

[98] Quoted in *Interreligious Dialogue*, 216.

[99] Quoted in *Interreligious Dialogue*, 277.

To a group of young Muslims in Morocco (1985): "The Catholic Church regards with respect and *recognizes the equality of your religious progress*, the richness of your spiritual tradition."[100]

This sampling of quotations is not intended to suggest that Pope John Paul II was a religious Pluralist who believed that many religions provide legitimate paths to Heaven. Instead they reflect the overall attitude of the pope, and all Moderate Inclusivists: while officially maintaining that Jesus is the only way to salvation, they are also quick to affirm their respect for other religions (not just the *members* of those religions), and to use language that could easily be understood in a pluralistic way.

For example, what are the young Muslims who heard the pope say that their "religious progress" was equal to that of Christians to think, other than that the pope endorses their practice of Islam? In the hundreds of statements directed to members of other religions put forth by Pope John Paul II during his pontificate, not once does he explicitly call on those persons to convert to Catholicism. It's difficult to interpret his words and actions in any way other than a belief that non-Catholics do not have to worry about their salvation.

For the Moderate Inclusivist, interreligious dialogue isn't about stating what Catholics believe and then listening to what other religions believe; it's about praising other religions unreservedly.

Expansive Inclusivists

Finally, a brief look at the most optimistic form of Inclusivism: Expansive Inclusivism. The Moderate Inclusivist is hopeful about

---

[100] Quoted in *Interreligious Dialogue*, 303, emphasis in original.

the salvation of non-Catholics, but the Expansive Inclusivist's hope is almost universalist. He takes the extraordinary means of salvation and seeks to make them ordinary. Rather than considering salvation as merely *possible* for non-Catholics, Expansive Inclusivists see it as probable, and construct theological systems to show exactly how this occurs. We've already mentioned the most famous such system: Karl Rahner's "Anonymous Christian" (see chapter 7).

It's important to note the two aspects of the theory of the Anonymous Christian. The first is that it retains the name "Christian." This is not Religious Pluralism, theologically speaking. It posits that anyone who is saved is saved through Christ (and therefore through the Church); this is still part of the Inclusivist camp. The "anonymous" aspect of the theory is what makes it an Expansive Inclusivist idea; it stretches the possibility of salvation to almost limitless boundaries.

If, as the Anonymous Christian theory posits, someone can actually be a Christian without any knowledge of Christ, simply by means of his or her conscience, then the possibility of salvation radically expands. Further, if there are many people — perhaps millions or even billions — who are in this way anonymously Christian, what is the purpose of missionary work? Why bother working to convert someone to something he already is, albeit anonymously? While all those in the Inclusivist camp have to grapple with the purpose of missionary work, for the Expansive Inclusivist, it's an insurmountable hurdle.

And it's not just missionary work that's impacted by the Expansive Inclusivist view. Why should anyone *remain* Catholic? If all I need to do is follow my conscience, then what is the purpose of the sacraments or being a member of the Church? If an "Anonymous Christian" can be saved, many Catholics reasonably ask, why should I bother to follow all the rules and regulations of Catholicism?

A few theologians take the Expansive Inclusivist view to its most extreme conclusion: perhaps it is possible for *everyone* to be saved. In his controversial book *Dare We Hope "That All Men Be Saved?"* prominent twentieth-century Catholic theologian Hans Urs von Balthasar argues that Catholics can have a reasonable hope that in the end every single person will be saved. Some critics of Balthasar incorrectly accuse him of Universalism, but that is not his theological position. He is not positing definitively that everyone *will* be saved, just that it's not impossible to hope that this will happen. Balthasar holds to the Inclusivist view that salvation comes through Christ and His Church, but his attitude is so overly hopeful as to include the possibility that *all* will be saved.

Balthasar's views appear radical in light of traditional Catholic teaching, yet he is embraced by many in the Church. He was a favorite of Pope John Paul II, who named him a cardinal (although Balthasar died two days before his investiture). More recently, his "reasonable hope" thesis has been embraced and promoted by Bishop Robert Barron, whose "Word on Fire" media empire has made him one of the most prominent American bishops in the Church today. Yet we've already seen that Pope Pius IX condemned this error when he added the erroneous belief, "Good hope at least is to be entertained of the eternal salvation of all those who are not at all in the true Church of Christ" to his *Syllabus of Errors*.[101] So although many Catholics today have embraced Balthasar's thesis, it was explicitly condemned before the Emphasis Shift.

[101] Pope Pius IX, *Syllabus of Errors*, 17.

In practice, we find most Expansive Inclusivists are no different than Pluralists. Both groups see salvation as possible for non-Catholics by way of their life choices, regardless of their religion. An interview Bishop Barron had with media personality Ben Shapiro in 2018 exemplifies how Expansive Inclusivism mirrors Pluralism.[102] In the interview, Shapiro, an Orthodox Jew, asks Barron:

> I feel like I lead a pretty good life, a very religiously based life in which I try to keep not just the Ten Commandments, but a solid 603 other commandments as well. And I spend an awful lot of my time promulgating what I would consider to be Judeo-Christian virtues, particularly in Western societies. So, what's the Catholic view of me? Am I basically screwed here?

Before getting to Barron's answer, let's imagine, based on what we've seen in chapters 2-4, how we think a Catholic bishop in 1920 or 1320 or A.D. 120 would answer this question from a practicing Jew. Although the tone might vary among those very different time periods, surely the answer would include the importance of being Catholic and would also include an explicit call to conversion. This call would be in keeping with the methodology of the greatest Catholic missionary of all time, St. Paul the Apostle, who continually called Jews to convert to Christ and His Church.

Barron, however, answers differently:

> No. The Catholic view—go back to the Second Vatican Council [which] says it very clearly. I mean, Christ is the

---

[102] Full interview found at "Bishop Robert Barron: The Ben Shapiro Show Sunday Special Ep. 31," Daily Wire YouTube Channel, https://youtu.be/0oDt8wWQsiA.

privileged route to salvation. "God so loved the world that He gave His only Son so that we may find eternal life," so that's the privileged route. However, Vatican II clearly teaches that someone outside the explicit Christian faith can be saved. Now, they're saved through the grace of Christ indirectly received, so I mean the grace is coming from Christ, but it might be received according to your conscience. So, if you're following your conscience sincerely, or in your case, you're following the commandments of the law sincerely, yeah, you can be saved.

Note the heart of the Expansive Inclusivist Barron's answer: Shapiro can be saved without converting. As an Inclusivist, Barron still notes that salvation would come through Christ, but his answer in no way promotes conversion as something Shapiro needs to undertake. Like most Inclusivists, however, Barron wants to distance his answer from a pluralistic, relativist view of religions:

Now, that doesn't conduce to a complete relativism. We still would say that the privileged route, and the route that God has offered to humanity, is the route of His Son, but no, you can be saved. Even Vatican II says [that] an atheist of good will can be saved ... when I follow my conscience, I'm following [Christ], whether I know it explicitly or not. So even the atheist, Vatican II teaches, of good will can be saved.

For the average person, particularly to the non-Christian like Shapiro, it's hard to distinguish Barron's answer from Religious Pluralism, even though Barron denies the similarity. First, Barron notes that Jesus is the "privileged route" to salvation, which implies Christ is not the *only* route. Other routes (perhaps including even atheism?) can lead to salvation as well, although Barron (and other Inclusivists) would say salvation still happens "through Christ" in some mysterious fashion. Second, the whole thrust of Barron's answer is to assuage any potential fears in Shapiro's (and other non-Christians') minds that Catholics think that non-Catholics might not go to Heaven. Barron's Expansive Inclusivist answer is full of presumption regarding the salvation of non-Catholics.

The Inclusivist school is by far the most dominant in the Church today. It contains a broad range of attitudes and theological premises; however, what unifies all members of the Inclusivist school is their overall hopefulness regarding the salvation of non-Catholics, whether they be non-Catholic Christians or non-Christians. Whether that optimism is somewhat tempered (the Reserved Inclusivists) or unguarded (the Expansive Inclusivists), practically speaking, the Inclusivists believe that most of those who are outside the visible boundaries of the Catholic Church are likely saved.

11

Many Paths to Heaven: The Pluralists

Members of the Inclusivist school, while being salvation opti‑
mists, insist that salvation can only come through Jesus Christ
and His Church. They accept EENS, but many — particularly
the Expansive Inclusivists — stretch the notion of "membership
in the Church" so far as to make it practically meaningless. Yet
they do not deny this perennial teaching.

However, after the Emphasis Shift, there arose some Catholic
theologians, including influential ones, who explicitly abandon
EENS. Instead of trying to walk the tightrope the Inclusivists
walk, they simply jump off, thereby putting themselves outside
official Church teaching. In spite of this, however, they are rarely
disciplined by Church authorities, and their views have become
the *de facto* belief of millions of Catholics worldwide. They are
the Religious Pluralists.

What is Religious Pluralism? It is the belief that many reli‑
gions can lead to salvation. Inclusivists believe that members
of other religions can obtain salvation, but that their salvation
still comes through Jesus Christ and His Church in some mys‑
terious fashion. The Catholic Church, in other words, is still
the means by which they are saved, even if the person is not

explicitly Catholic. Pluralists, however, say that other religions can themselves be the means by which a person is saved.

To the average person, those two positions might seem like a distinction without a difference. And it's true that the line between a Pluralist and an Inclusivist (particularly an Expansive Inclusivist) is blurry. After all, what's the difference, practically speaking, between a devout Muslim who dies as a Muslim and is saved in some unknown fashion through the Church, and a devout Muslim who dies as a Muslim and is saved through his practice of Islam?

Herein lies the problem with the Inclusivist school: it essentially embraces the Pluralist position in practice, while dancing around theological issues so that it maintains, at least in theory, acceptance of magisterial teaching. But the theological nuances usually don't trickle down to the average Catholic; he just understands that one does not have to be Catholic to be saved, and so for him, one religion is as good as another. Even though most theologians or bishops or priests may belong to the Inclusivist school, and officially teach the Inclusivist view, the end result is that most lay Catholics become religious Pluralists. Remember the 2014 Pew Study[103] I previously noted that found 68 percent of Catholics believe that non-Christian religions can lead to eternal life. That's Religious Pluralism.

Let us look, then, a bit more deeply at how Pluralism went from being a condemned heresy to the *de facto* belief of most Catholics.

Vatican II and Pluralism

As with most of the common conceptions in the Church today, we have to go back to Vatican II to find Pluralism's foundations.

---

[103] Pew Research Center, "U.S. Public Becoming Less Religious."

To be clear, Vatican II did *not* teach Pluralism, but its language helped lead to an embrace of Pluralism by many Catholics. It did this by stressing that salvation can come to those outside the visible Catholic Church.

Gaudium et Spes (the Pastoral Constitution on the Church in the Modern World), one of the most important documents from the Council, notes that Christians are "linked with the paschal mystery," and then states,

> All this holds true not only for Christians, but for all men of good will in whose hearts grace works in an unseen way. For, since Christ died for all men, and since the ultimate vocation of man is in fact one, and divine, we ought to believe that the Holy Spirit *in a manner known only to God* offers to every man the possibility of being associated with this paschal mystery.[104]

Addressing the Church's missionary activity, another Vatican II document, *Ad Gentes*, uses similar language:

> Though God *in ways known to Himself* can lead those inculpably ignorant of the Gospel to find that faith without which it is impossible to please Him (Heb. 11:6), yet a necessity lies upon the Church (1 Cor. 9:16), and at the same time a sacred duty, to preach the Gospel.[105]

In both cases, Vatican II speaks of salvation coming to non-Christians in ways "known only to God." Further, *Gaudium et Spes* notes that the Holy Spirit is active outside the visible bonds of the Church, creating the possibility of salvation for those outside it.

---

[104] *Gaudium et Spes*, 22, emphasis added.
[105] *Ad Gentes*, 7, emphasis added.

Although the texts do not say that the Holy Spirit will work through the practice of other religions, they do not preclude that possibility, either.

Further, when mentioning other religions, the Vatican II texts are exceedingly positive, including their references to other religions' rituals and practices. *Lumen Gentium*, for example, speaks of "whatever good lies latent in the *religious practices and cultures* of diverse peoples,"[106] implying that the practice of other religions can be "good." In *Ad Gentes*, the Council fathers suggest that some elements of other religions are the working of the Holy Spirit, stating that "whatever truth and grace are to be found among the nations" are "a sort of secret presence of God."[107]

Another Vatican II document, *Nostra Aetate*, the Declaration on the Relation of the Church to Non-Christian Religions, also pushes a positive outlook on other religions. When speaking of Hinduism and Buddhism — religions radically different from Catholicism — *Nostra Aetate* states,

> The Catholic Church rejects nothing that is true and holy in these religions. She regards with sincere reverence those ways of conduct and of life, those precepts and teachings which, though differing in many aspects from the ones she holds and sets forth, nonetheless often reflect a ray of that Truth which enlightens all men.[108]

To reiterate, Vatican II does not explicitly endorse Religious Pluralism in these texts. It regards other religions as a "preparation" for the Gospel. In other words, the elements of truth

---

[106] *Lumen Gentium*, 17, emphasis added.
[107] *Ad Gentes*, 9.
[108] *Nostra Aetate*, 2.

found in other religions—which find their source in the Holy Spirit—help prepare non-Christians for the Gospel. This is also the position held by Popes Paul VI, John Paul II (especially), and Benedict XVI. However, Vatican II's emphasis on the Spirit working in other religions and the Council's focus on the positive elements of those religions prepares Catholics for the acceptance of Religious Pluralism.

From Inclusivism to Pluralism: The Case of Hans Küng

Although Vatican II does not espouse Pluralism, it does embrace Inclusivism. This Inclusivism becomes a gateway for the adoption of Pluralism by many Catholics. In most cases, this is simply a matter of average Catholics who do not understand the nuanced theological differences between Inclusivism and Pluralism. But Inclusivist theologians also evolved into Pluralists. None was more prominent than Hans Küng, the story of whom presents a case study for the growth of Pluralism in the Church.

Hans Küng is one of the most significant Catholic theologians of the twentieth century. Ordained a priest in 1954, the early 1960s find him a professor of theology at the University of Tübingen in Germany when he is selected by Pope John XXIII as a *peritus* (theological advisor) at Vatican II. In his long career he has advanced many controversial ideas, including a rejection of papal infallibility. Although the Church strips him of his license to teach Catholic theology in 1979, he continues to be an influential voice in the Church.

It's unknown what Küng's interreligious outlook was before Vatican II, as we have none of his writings on the topic from that time. The default position before Vatican II was, of course, Exclusivism, but Tübingen was known as a hotbed for liberalism, so it's possible that even before Vatican II Küng embraced Inclusivism. We do know that in an address he gave in 1964 in Bombay he rejects the idea that "non-believers" (meaning non-Christians) are automatically damned. He argues that Christianity is the "normative" revelation of God, but that those who don't know Christ can also be saved. So by this time Küng was already an Expansive Inclusivist.

Over the next few decades, Küng continues to teach his Expansive Inclusivist approach. In his 1974 book *On Being a Christian* he harshly condemns the Exclusivist view and gives lavish praise for other religions while maintaining that Christianity is distinctive among them. Küng's embrace of the value of other religions is met with resistance from more Reserved Inclusivists (and of course by Exclusivists), but perhaps surprisingly it is also criticized by full-fledged Pluralists. In 1981, Paul Knitter, a prominent Pluralist theologian, criticizes Küng for not going far enough on the Salvation Spectrum. He accuses Küng of focusing on Christ's uniqueness and depending too much on the Christian Scriptures for his arguments.

Küng appears to take Knitter's criticisms to heart because in the 1980s we see his metamorphosis from Expansive Inclusivist to Pluralist.[109] In his 1985 book *Christianity and the World Religions* Küng looks to other religions—particularly Islam, Hinduism, and Buddhism—as the most able to address the needs of the modern world. His emphasis on the distinctiveness of Christianity is nearly gone, as are his previous (muted) criticisms of other religions. He writes,

> If God is truly the Absolute, then he is all these things in one: Nirvana, insofar as he is the goal of the way of

---

[109] See Scott Cowdell, "Hans Küng and World Religions: The Emergence of a Pluralist," *Theology* 92, no. 746 (1989).

salvation; dharma, insofar as he is the law that shapes the cosmos and humanity; emptiness, insofar as he forever eludes all affirmative determinations; and the primal Buddha, insofar as he is the origin of everything that exists.[110]

By the mid-1980s, then, Küng has evolved into a religious Pluralist, no longer bound to maintaining even a tenuous connection to official Catholic teaching as Inclusivists do.

The *De Facto* View

Why does it matter what Hans Küng, a Swiss theologian who's not even allowed to teach Catholic theology, thinks? It matters because Küng's personal evolution represents an evolution in the thinking of millions of Catholics since the 1960s. While most Church leaders and most Catholic theologians maintain an officially Inclusivist concept of salvation, a majority of Catholics (68 percent, according to the Pew study) embrace a Pluralist view.

Many studies have shown this reality, and so has a plethora of anecdotal evidence. In my years as a diocesan director of evangelization, I spoke with many "pew-sitter" Catholics. These were Catholics who attended Mass regularly and took their faith seriously enough to attend talks on Catholicism outside of Mass. The presentations I gave emphasized the uniqueness and importance of Catholicism, yet more times than I could count attendees made a point of telling me that as long as their friends/family were "good Muslims" or "good Protestants," then surely God would bring them to Heaven. Any religion—even no religion—was fine, as long as the person was sincere in his beliefs, no matter

---

[110] Hans Küng, *Christianity and World Religions* (Garden City, NY: Collins, 1987), 392-393.

what those beliefs were. The nuances of being saved through the Church even though one is a Muslim (the Inclusivist view) were lost.

This widespread attitude is not a surprise. Most Catholics have repeatedly heard the Expansive Inclusivist view — that we should be optimistic about the salvation of most people, no matter their religion — from most Church leaders most of the time. Practically speaking, then, most Catholics take the same path as Küng, although perhaps with fewer theological nuances. Inclusivism in theory leads to Pluralism in practice.

But Pluralism isn't the final stop. When a person believes that all religions are essentially equal, and that the practice of any of them leads to the same eternal destination, then naturally he becomes indifferent to what religion others practice, or even if they practice any religion at all. He also becomes indifferent to his own religion, and when he hits a roadblock in his practice of Catholicism, he questions whether it's worth it to try to overcome that roadblock. Religion becomes, at best, a cultural force which some enjoy practicing and others do not. So while Inclusivism leads to Pluralism, Pluralism leads to indifference. And indifference has emptied the pews.

12

Defending the Tradition: The Exclusivists

After the Emphasis Shift, Inclusivism becomes the predominant position of Church leaders, and through Inclusivism, Pluralism creeps into the minds and hearts of millions of pew-sitting Catholics. But what about the school that dominated the Church from its inception until the 1960s? What about Exclusivism?

Exclusivism is sent to the catacombs. It quickly becomes a tiny minority view in the Church after the 1960s, isolated to certain fringe quarters. Initially only critics of Vatican II, such as Archbishop Marcel Lefebvre, founder of the Society of St. Pius X, remained Exclusivists. Today it is the self-described "traditionalists" who make up the majority of the small Exclusivist school, but we'll see that some Catholics who do not identify as traditionalists have also embraced Exclusivism.

Keeping the Old Emphasis

What differentiates the Exclusivists from the Inclusivists? After all, in the Salvation Spectrum they both fall in the box that delineates Catholic teaching. Isn't that all that matters? No. Although it is attitude more than theology that distinguishes the two schools (although nuances in theology shape those attitudes), the difference in attitude has major practical ramifications.

Many Inclusivists consider Exclusivists part of the Absolutist school, but this is inaccurate. When it comes to conformity to official Church teaching, both Inclusivists and Exclusivists accept that individuals can be saved even if they are not baptized members of the visible Catholic Church (as opposed to Absolutists, who insist only water-baptized Catholics have any chance at salvation). For example, the Exclusivist Lefebvre wrote in 1968, just three years after Vatican II ended,

> Does that mean that no Protestant, no Muslim, no Buddhist or animist will be saved? No, it would be a second error to think that. Those who cry for intolerance in interpreting St. Cyprian's formula, "Outside the Church there is no salvation," also reject the Creed, "I confess one baptism for the remission of sins," and are insufficiently instructed as to what baptism is. There are three ways of receiving it: the baptism of water; the baptism of blood (that of the martyrs who confessed the faith while still catechumens) and baptism of desire.[111]

Obviously Lefebvre does not reject magisterial Church teaching, repeatedly expressed by the Church before the 1960s, that both Baptism of blood and Baptism of desire are legitimate, if extraordinary, means of salvation. Lefebvre even elucidates the teaching first expressed by Pope Pius IX, that one's desire to be baptized can be *implicit*:

---

[111] Archbishop Marcel Lefebvre, *Open Letter to Confused Catholics*, chap. 10, "Ecumenism," http://www.sspxasia.com/Documents/ Archbishop-Lefebvre/OpenLetterToConfusedCatholics/Chapter -10.htm.

The doctrine of the Church also recognizes implicit baptism of desire. This consists in doing the will of God. God knows all men and He knows that amongst Protestants, Muslims, Buddhists and in the whole of humanity there are men of good will. They receive the grace of baptism without knowing it, but in an effective way. In this way they become part of the Church.[112]

Based on these quotes alone, one cannot discern any difference between Lefebvre and the Inclusivist school. However, what makes Lefebvre an Exclusivist is his attitude toward the extraordinary means of salvation, particularly the implicit Baptism of desire. He does not emphasize them, and does not presume that they are likely for most people. Unlike the Inclusivists, he is no salvation optimist:

But at the cost of what difficulties do people in those countries where Christianity has not penetrated come to receive baptism by desire! Error is an obstacle to the Holy Ghost. This explains why the Church has always sent missionaries into all countries of the world, why thousands of them have suffered martyrdom. If salvation can be found in any religion, why cross the seas, why subject oneself to unhealthy climates, to a harsh life, to sickness and an early death? From the martyrdom of St. Stephen onwards (the first to give his life for Christ, and for this reason his feast is the day after Christmas), the Apostles set out to spread the Good News throughout the Mediterranean countries.[113]

Lefebvre, who was himself a missionary in Africa for many years, does not believe it is easy for a non-Catholic to implicitly

[112] Lefebvre, *Open Letter*, chap. 10.
[113] Lefebvre, *Open Letter*, chap. 10.

desire Baptism, or at the very least, Catholics should never assume a non-Catholic has done so. While it might be true that a "good person" who isn't Catholic can make it to Heaven, the Exclusivist believes that such a scenario is likely rare; it's truly extra-ordinary. Most importantly, the Exclusivist doesn't think it's up to man to apply the extraordinary means; only God alone can do that. These means cannot therefore be presumed to apply in a given situation.

A main reason for the Exclusivist's attitude is his acknowledgement of the impact of Original Sin. Because Original Sin has caused all men to be attracted to evil—and to tend away from God, rather than toward Him—we need the graces of the sacraments and the teachings of the Church to overcome that. To do this in a situation that doesn't include these things is extremely difficult.

Further, Exclusivists take seriously the words of Jesus, "Enter by the narrow gate; for the gate is wide and the way is easy, that leads to destruction, and those who enter by it are many. For the gate is narrow and the way is hard, that leads to life, and those who find it are few" (Matt. 7:13-14). That's the real crux of the Exclusivist position: Catholics should assume that non-Catholics are *not* going to be saved and pray and work for their conversion. If, in fact, God does in the end save them without their being members of the visible Church, that is part of His merciful plan. But it would be the sin of presumption to act as if they were already saved.

Exclusivists concentrate on *our* obligations. We are obligated to be baptized and live as visible members of the Church, and to call others to do likewise. According to the Exclusivist, we should not fixate on what it's possible for *God* to do—the extraordinary means of salvation. Doing so obscures our own obligations.

All Religions Should Be Treated Equally?

Another way in which many Exclusivists differ from Inclusivists (and Pluralists) is that they are more skeptical of the concept of religious liberty. The Vatican II document *Dignitatis Humanae* declared unequivocally that "the human person has a right to religious freedom."[114] All theologians acknowledge this constitutes a change from the Church's historic view of the role of the State regarding religion. Many Exclusivists believe this was a change in the wrong direction.

Bishop Athanasius Schneider, auxiliary bishop of the Archdiocese of Saint Mary in Astana, Kazakhstan, and a leading worldwide voice for more traditional Catholic practices, has called into question the wisdom of *Dignitatis Humanae*. He believes it fosters a spirit of religious indifference and that it can be used to promote religious error:

> However, with ... *Dignitatis Humanae*, there was in my opinion a drastic change regarding the previous and universal Magisterium of the Church, which had always said that error does not have the same right as truth to be propagated. Error has no rights by nature, just as we have no right by nature to sin.[115]

Schneider does not support coercing people to Catholicism, and he acknowledges that a society must have toleration for other religions ("Catholics must tolerate even erroneous religions in view of the common good"[116]), but all religions should not be treated as equal by the State. Instead, it should prefer Catholicism:

[114] *Dignitatis Humanae*, 2.
[115] Schneider, *Christus Vincit*, 86.
[116] Schneider, *Christus Vincit*, 85.

The state, of course, should not interfere in Church affairs. However, as representatives of the people, they must publicly worship Christ, the true God, and practice the true religion, which is only the Catholic religion. This is the constant Catholic truth, which no ecclesiastical authority can change into its contrary.[117]

To the Exclusivist, the emphasis on Catholicism as the one and only religion should impact even governments. To treat all religions as equal is to endorse a pluralistic view that fosters indifference.

Further, Exclusivists spurn the practice common today among Church leaders to speak only positively about other religions. They are willing to state flatly that non-Catholic religions are false religions and point out ways in which they are contrary to the natural law or divine revelation. In addition, Exclusivists do not downplay or hide the uniqueness of Catholicism; they emphasize it.

Bishop Schneider, for example, writes:

It is false to say that God works with His sanctifying grace in non-Christians through a "sacramental dimension."[118] When God works in non-Christians, He does so by other means which only He knows and which we do not know. "Signs and rites" as sacred expressions pleasing to God are found only in the new and everlasting covenant in the Church, which God Himself established. *Outside the Church there are no salvific and religious rites pleasing to God* ... The very existence of [non-Christian religions] is contrary to the will of God.[119]

---

[117] Schneider, *Christus Vincit*, 87.

[118] Note: This is a phrase used in Pope Francis's encyclical *Evangelii Gaudium* (2013), 254.

[119] Schneider, *Christus Vincit*, 90-91, emphasis added.

Exclusivists are heavily critical of both the ecumenical movement and particularly the interreligious dialogue movement. They would have Catholicism promoted and the errors of non-Catholic religions pointed out and condemned.

Vatican II Was Exclusivist?

Naturally, most Exclusivists are more traditional overall in their religious views, and many are critics of Vatican II, which we have seen opened the floodgates for Inclusivism and even Pluralism in the Church. Yet not all Exclusivists fit into that mold. Ralph Martin, a professor of theology at Sacred Heart Major Seminary and a leader in the charismatic Catholic movement, argues that the Exclusivist view is compatible with Vatican II and, in fact, is the proper reading of the Vatican II documents.

Martin's 2012 book *Will Many Be Saved? What Vatican II Actually Teaches and Its Implications for the New Evangelization*[120] argues that the "salvation optimism" that flowed from the Council was not in keeping with the documents themselves. He examines in particular *Lumen Gentium* 16, which describes the relationship of non-Christians to the "people of God." Martin claims that this key passage is misinterpreted by Inclusivists.

The key phrase from *Lumen Gentium* that engenders "salvation optimism" is the following:

> But the plan of salvation also includes those who acknowledge the Creator. In the first place amongst these there are the Muslims, who, professing to hold the faith of Abraham,

---

[120] Ralph Martin, *Will Many Be Saved? What Vatican II Actually Teaches and Its Implications for the New Evangelization* (Grand Rapids, MI: William Eerdmans, 2012).

along with us adore the one and merciful God, who on the last day will judge mankind. Nor is God far distant from those who in shadows and images seek the unknown God, for it is He who gives to all men life and breath and all things, and as Saviour wills that all men be saved. Those also can attain to salvation who through no fault of their own do not know the Gospel of Christ or His Church, yet sincerely seek God and moved by grace strive by their deeds to do His will as it is known to them through the dictates of conscience. Nor does Divine Providence deny the helps necessary for salvation to those who, without blame on their part, have not yet arrived at an explicit knowledge of God and with His grace strive to live a good life.[121]

This passage is the foundation for an optimistic view regarding the salvation of non-Christians, a view the dominant Inclusivist school has embraced since the Council. Yet Martin says that this passage from *Lumen Gentium* 16 must be balanced with the concluding sentences of that paragraph:

But often men, deceived by the Evil One, have become vain in their reasonings and have exchanged the truth of God for a lie, serving the creature rather than the Creator. Or some there are who, living and dying in this world without God, are exposed to final despair. Wherefore to promote the glory of God and procure the salvation of all of these, and mindful of the command of the Lord, "Preach the Gospel to every creature," the Church fosters the missions with care and attention.

[121] *Lumen Gentium*, 16.

The underlying Latin translated here (using the Vatican web-site translation) as "But often" is *at saepius*. Another translation renders it as "But rather often" (the Walter Abbot 1966 translation), and another commonly used translation (the Austin Flannery 1996 translation) reads "Very often." Martin uses the "very often" translation — a translation that implies the rarity of someone outside the Church *not* being "deceived by the Evil One." Regarding the passage as a whole, Martin argues that these sentences should be a restraining force on any overly hopeful view of salvation. In particular, this passage should cause Catholics to reject Inclusivist theories such as Rahner's "Anonymous Christian" or Balthasar's hope that all men might be saved.

In an interview Martin explains how *Lumen Gentium* 16, and in a sense the entire Council, should be properly understood:

> The Council has a very clear teaching that is virtually unknown and would really bring a solution to this confusion and ill-founded presumption. It is contained in the *Constitution on the Church*, Section 16.
>
> What the Council here teaches is that, under certain conditions, it is possible for people who have never heard the Gospel to be saved. The conditions are:
> 1. That they are inculpably ignorant.
> 2. That they are sincerely seeking to know God, who reveals himself in some measure through the creation and through the light of conscience.
> 3. That they are trying to live in accordance with the light of conscience, assisted by God's grace.
>
> People hear this teaching and, very strangely, often jump to the conclusion that these conditions are probably generally fulfilled and so most people are saved; indeed,

without hearing the Gospel. But this is a false conclusion and is contradicted by the last three sentences of *Lumen Gentium*, 16. Karl Rahner in his work on this issue ignores the last three sentences. Balthasar ignores them, as well . . .

The Council is [in the last three sentences of *Lumen Gentium* 16] reminding us that no one lives in a neutral environment and that the world, the flesh and the devil are powerful forces leading people away from saying "Yes" to the grace of God. The Council here is reminding us that even though it is theoretically possible for people who have not heard the Gospel to be saved, it is very difficult, and, very often, it does not happen; and so we need to urgently carry out the work of evangelization.[122]

We have here again the crux of the Exclusivist position: it is "very difficult" for a person who has not heard the Gospel to be saved, and we must not presume someone will be saved by the extraordinary means available. Rather we should work to share the Gospel with him so that he can be saved via the ordinary means.

Even if Exclusivists disagree about whether Vatican II endorses the Inclusivist position or not, they agree that the Inclusivist position is *not* the view embraced by the Church for the nearly two thousand years leading up to the Council.

Exclusivism and Religious Indifference

The Exclusivists and Inclusivists share many theological views: both hold that salvation is *possible* for those outside the visible

---

[122] Edward Pentin, "Ralph Martin on Salvation of Souls: 'Urgently Carry Out the Work of Evangelization,'" *National Catholic Register*, October 10, 2019, https://www.ncregister.com/daily-news/ralph-martin-on-salvation-of-souls-urgently-carry-out-the-work-of-evangeliz.

boundaries of the Catholic Church; however, they disagree about whether we can speculate if such salvation is *likely*. While this might seem like a minor difference, it has immense ramifications. Unlike Inclusivism, Exclusivism does not lead to religious indifference. It does not lead to a collapse in the missions. It reminds Catholics that they have a vital reason to remain Catholic — their very salvation depends upon it. Exclusivism urges Catholics to practice their own faith and to engage in missionary work, for Exclusivists know that all religions are *not* equal, and practicing another religion does not help one get to Heaven. As Martin notes,

> The Decree on Non-Christian Religions [*Nostra Aetate*], while not denying the need to evangelize and call members of these religions to Christ, was also destabilizing. Up until the very eve of Vatican II, the papal encyclicals on mission emphasized the defects in the world religions, including idolatry and Satanic elements, and issued strong calls to mission for the sake of their salvation. The Decree on Non-Christian Religions now emphasized certain commonalities and recognized rays of truth and seeds of the Gospel present in these non-Christian religions. *This again led to many people surmising that, since this is the case, perhaps there is no need for evangelization, since people can be saved without hearing the Gospel.* This was explicitly taught in *Lumen Gentium*, 16, but the grave difficulties in this being the case were almost never averted to.[123]

Bishop Schneider also laments the impact of Inclusivism (and Pluralism) on the missionary work of the Church:

[123] Pentin, "Ralph Martin on Salvation of Souls."

The confusion spread by incorrect interreligious events and discussions is one of the deepest crises in the Church today. In some ways, it is a betrayal of Christ. Practically, and hopefully not intentionally, Christ is put on the same level with other religions. *This implies a loss of real missionary zeal which inspired the Apostles, the Church Fathers, and the great missionary saints.* We have an urgent need to return to this missionary zeal. The lack of zeal is a deep wound in the Church. This is the question of all times: either Christ or nothing. The uniqueness of Christ and His Church is the core of the entire Gospel. Truly, we must return to the Catholic missionary zeal of all times.[124]

Exclusivism regards an emphasis on the ordinary means of salvation as essential to keeping Catholics in the Church and encouraging non-Catholics to convert. In an age when millions of Catholics are leaving and few converts are being made, Exclusivists want to recover the lost passion for Catholicism and the missionary zeal of previous generations. They want to give people a driving reason to remain or become Catholic. Exclusivists argue that this is done not by changing Catholic doctrine, but by changing attitudes — by changing our "salvation optimism" to a more realistic view of the possibility of salvation for non-Catholics. It means highlighting the ordinary means of salvation and putting them at the forefront of our teaching and missionary work. However, for now at least, this marks them as a small, fringe minority in the Church.

---

[124] Schneider, *Christus Vincit*, 104, emphasis added.

IV. The Practical Aftermath

As we've determined, multiple schools of theological thought — including the Universalist, Pluralist, and Inclusivist schools — fostered a spirit of indifference among Catholics following the Emphasis Shift. But it isn't just ivory tower theology debates that have an influence in the pews. It is also the actions of Church leaders, particularly their interactions with non-Catholics.

The goals of the Church's ecumenical and interreligious outreach underwent a radical alteration after the Emphasis Shift. Before the 1960s, Church leaders put little to no effort toward either ecumenism or interreligious dialogue. When it came to non-Catholic Christians, Church leaders desired reunification with them inside the Catholic Church; the goal was Christian unity under the bishop of Rome, the pope. When it came to non-Christians, the Church's aim was conversion to Catholicism via missionary work. In both cases, the objective was clear-cut (and essentially the same for Christians and non-Christians): conversion to Catholicism.

Now these goals are jettisoned, replaced by calls for a vague "full communion" among all Christians, and "mutual understanding" between Christians and non-Christians. Imagine if Microsoft left the computing sector to focus on making toiletry products—that's how radical the Church's goal-shifting was. Every aspect of Church life was questioned and revised to meet these new missions. Ecumenism and interreligious dialogue, not conversion, become the driving force of the Church's outreach.

13

The Church of Ecumenism

The most immediate practical impact of the Church's Emphasis Shift is the rise of ecumenical activity within the Church. Ecumenism, remember, is the term used for the Church's relations with non-Catholic Christians (*not* with non-Christians). We've noted that the modern ecumenical movement began in earnest in the early twentieth century among Protestant Christians. Protestantism had endured disunity in doctrine and practice since its very founding; by the twentieth century many Protestants wanted to work to end that disunity. The Catholic Church, however, already believing herself to be the one united Church of Christ, was wary of and even opposed to this movement. The only action Church leaders took toward the ecumenical movement at that time was to call non-Catholic Christians to return to the already-united Catholic Church.

After the Emphasis Shift, however, the Church embraces the new goal of "full communion" between all Christians, although what that "full communion" represents remains ambiguous. Now Church leaders desire to work side-by-side with non-Catholic Christians to achieve a shared goal: a future united Church of Christ which transcends the Catholic Church. This new presumption pervades the ecumenical activities and dialogues of

Catholics and shapes how Catholics perceive other Christian communities and—crucially—their own Catholic Faith.

Subsisting in Ambiguity

In chapter 7 I noted the importance of the controversial phrase "subsists in" in the Vatican II document, *Lumen Gentium*: "The one Church of Christ ... constituted and organized in the world as a society, *subsists in* the Catholic Church."[125] Instead of stating that the "Church of Christ *is* the Catholic Church" (the word previous Church documents used), *Lumen Gentium* replaces "is" with "subsists in." One cannot overstate the impact this simple change in phrasing has had on ecumenical relations. This simple phrase gives the theological foundation for the new approach to non-Catholic Christians: instead of calling them to return, Catholics must walk side-by-side with them to achieve a still-to-be-realized united Church of Christ.

How do "subsists in" and "is" differ? By interchanging these phrases with other objects, we can see the difference between them more clearly. For example, consider the following:

- Fruit-ness is apples.
- Fruit-ness subsists in apples.

In the first statement, there is an identity between fruit-ness and apples. In other words, only apples exemplify fruit-ness; i.e., there are no other fruits, and to be an apple is the only way to be a fruit. The second statement, however, more accurately describes reality—that apples are fruits, but there are other objects in the world that have fruit-ness, such as oranges and bananas. Generally stated, if object A subsists in object B, then object A can also exist elsewhere. Object B is greater than just object A; there

---

[125] *Lumen Gentium*, 8, emphasis added.

can be other, equally valid objects that also subsist in object B. "Subsists in" and "is" do *not* mean the same thing.

So, if the Church of Christ *is* the Catholic Church, then the two can be identified as the same entity. But if the Church of Christ merely *subsists in* the Catholic Church, then the Church of Christ exists elsewhere in some manner. The difference between the two has a major impact on the goal of ecumenism. If the Church of Christ is the Catholic Church, then for Catholics the goal of ecumenism is the conversion of non-Catholics to that Church of Christ, which is the Catholic Church. But if the Church of Christ subsists in the Catholic Church, then perhaps Catholics need to work with non-Catholic Christians toward that Church of Christ which, although it subsists in the Catholic Church, also somehow transcends her.

Soon after Vatican II ends, Gérard Philips, the primary drafter of *Lumen Gentium*, predicts that the "subsists in" expression will "cause floods of ink to flow."[126] He is right: "subsists in" becomes the flashpoint for understanding and practicing ecumenism. Apparently it is easy for Philips to make his prediction, because "subsists in" was deliberately chosen for its ambiguity and openness to multiple interpretations: when asked why this phrase was used, Philips said, "we wanted to keep the matter open."[127]

Due to this planned ambiguity, "subsists in" becomes a theological Rorschach Test: Catholic theologians project their own views of ecumenism onto the phrase. While some insist "subsists

---

[126] Francis A. Sullivan, S.J., "Quaestio Disputata the Meaning of *Subsistit in* as Explained by the Congregation for the Doctrine of the Faith," *Theological Studies* 69, no. 1 (February 2008): 116.

[127] John Wilkins, "The 'Straight Arrow' Theologian and the Pope," *National Catholic Reporter*, November 12, 2010, https://www.ncronline.org/news/people/straight-arrow-theologian-and-pope.

in" means the same thing as "is," many others see it as opening up new understandings of what it means to be the Church of Christ, and who is a member of that Church. According to one common interpretation, it means that the Church of Christ subsists in *other* churches or denominations (like other fruits subsist in fruit-ness), and these belief systems are therefore as valid as the Catholic Church.

One influential promoter of this interpretation is Leonardo Boff, a Brazilian theologian and former Franciscan priest (he left the priesthood in 1992). In the early 1980s he published a book titled *Church: Charism and Power*. In it Boff denies that Christ founded a Church; rather, Boff insists that the Church evolved on her own. He argues that the one true Church therefore is not limited to a particular expression and that the phrase "subsists in" shows that the Catholic Church is simply one expression of the true Church. "In fact it (sc. the sole Church of Christ) may also be present in other Christian Churches."[128] Boff's teachings became so influential that the Congregation of the Doctrine of the Faith (then headed by Cardinal Joseph Ratzinger, the future Pope Benedict XVI) felt the need to publicly intervene. In its 1985 *Notification on the book 'Church: Charism and Power,'* the CDF rejects Boff's interpretation of "subsists in" and argues that there is only one "subsistence" of the true Church, which is the Catholic Church.

This intervention of the CDF came a full twenty years after the end of Vatican II, and by then the genie was out of the bottle.

---

[128] Leonardo Boff, *Church, Charism and Power: Liberation Theology and the Institutional Church* (Spring Valley, NY: Crossroad Publishing, 1986), 75. Cf. Brian Kusek, "Subsistit In: Full Identity or Discontinuity?" (2016), pp. 47-48. *School of Divinity Master's Theses and Projects* 16, https://ir.stthomas.edu/sod_mat/16.

"Subsists in" played a fundamental role in the Emphasis Shift among Catholic theologians, dramatically impacting not only ecumenical relations but Catholics' understanding of the Church. This view trickled down to the average Catholic layperson. For example, one of the most influential Catholic books in the United States in the 1980s was Richard McBrien's *Catholicism*. Countless American Catholics were formed by this text. Presented as a kind of catechism for "mature" Catholics, *Catholicism* includes many elements that conflict with traditional Catholic teachings, including a depiction of the Church based on McBrien's understanding of the language of "subsists in." McBrien writes:

> [The] Church ... embraces more than the Catholic Church. It is the whole Body of Christ: Catholics, Orthodox, Anglicans, and Protestants alike. This principle is to be found in the *Decree of Ecumenism* and in the *Dogmatic Constitution on the Church* (*Lumen gentium*) [note: where the "subsists in" language is found]. It sets aside the pre-Vatican II concept that the Roman Catholic Church alone is the one, true Church, and that other Christian communities ... are somehow "related" to the Church but are not real members of it.[129]

McBrien's definition of the "Church," therefore, includes *all* Christian communities. Later McBrien gives a definition of the Church in which he notes, "This definition embraces all Christians: Catholics, Orthodox, Anglicans, and Protestants. Thus, although the noun *Church* is singular, it is always to be understood at the same time as having a pluralistic character.

---

[129] Richard P. McBrien, *Catholicism*, vol. 2 (Minneapolis: Winston Press, 1980), 685.

There is always 'the Church' and there are 'the churches.'"[130] In other words, the Church of Christ subsists in the Catholic Church, but it also subsists in some form in every other Christian community. It follows that Christian communities other than the Catholic Church can also be a means of salvation in Christ. The Catholic Church becomes, in effect, just another Christian denomination. This opinion, presented in this highly popular text and held by many Catholic theologians other than McBrien, comes to dominate the outlook of the average Catholic.

Not just liberal but conservative Catholic theologians are also influenced by the language of "subsists in." Avery Cardinal Dulles, a prominent American conservative theologian who passed away in 2008, defended the phrase against liberal attempts to paint the Catholic Church as simply one church among many. Yet even he admitted that the phrase implies that "Vatican II looks upon the Church of Christ as transcending Roman Catholicism."[131]

The CDF issues not one, not two, but three separate documents over the years trying to clarify what "subsists in" really means. In addition to the 1985 notification about Boff's book, it also issues *Dominus Iesus* in 2000 to address the phrase, and in 2007 it releases *Responses to Some Questions Regarding Certain Aspects of the Doctrine on the Church*, which directly answers the questions, "What is the meaning of the affirmation that the Church of Christ subsists in the Catholic Church?" and "Why was the expression 'subsists in' adopted instead of the simple word 'is'?" This document is intended to be the final word on the meaning of the infamous phrase.

---

[130] McBrien, *Catholicism*, vol. 2, 714.

[131] Avery Dulles, "The Church, the Churches, and the Catholic Church," *Theological Studies* 33, no. 2 (May 1972): 211.

Yet even with these official clarifications, the impact of the phrase permanently alters Catholic understanding of the nature of the Catholic Church and of ecumenism. After the release of *Dominus Iesus*, Walter Cardinal Kasper, one of the leading Catholic ecumenists in the world and at the time the President of the Pontifical Council for Promoting Christian Unity, wrote:

> Even if [*Dominus Iesus's*] understanding of "subsistit" does not resolve all the questions, it offers us a solid basis for ecumenical dialogue. The first consequence of the thesis that the one church of Jesus Christ subsists in the Catholic Church is that at the present unity is not only given in fragments, and would therefore be a future ecumenical goal. Rather, unity also subsists in the Catholic Church; it is already real in it. *This does not mean that full communion as the goal of the ecumenical way has to be understood simply as the return of separated brothers and churches to the bosom of the Catholic mother church. In the situation of division, unity in the Catholic Church is not concretely realised in all its fullness; the divisions remain a wound for the Catholic Church too.*[132]

Historically, Catholics desired that non-Catholic Christians become Catholic. That was the means to Christian unity. For Kasper and other Catholic ecumenists, however, "subsists in" shifts the goal. Since the Catholic Church is not identified with the Church of Christ, the goal of ecumenism is to find a unity that

---

[132] Walter Cardinal Kasper, "Communio: The Guiding Concept of Catholic Ecumenical Theology," *Unita Dei Christia* (November 2002): 10, http://www.foerderverein-unita-dei-cristiani.com/seite/pdf/wk_communio.pdf (emphasis added).

exists beyond the Catholic Church's current unity, nebulously defined as "full communion."

Striving for "Full Communion"

Like "subsists in," the phrase "full communion" also transforms Catholic ecumenical relations. *Unitatis Redintegratio*, the Vatican II decree on ecumenism, states:

> Nevertheless, the divisions among Christians prevent the Church from attaining the fullness of catholicity proper to her, in those of her sons who, though attached to her by Baptism, are yet *separated from full communion with her*.[133]

Three more times the decree mentions "full communion" as something that has been lost and needs to be restored.

This phrase, "full communion," is a new one in the history of the Church, selected by the Council fathers to emphasize that while non-Catholic Christians are not visible members of the Catholic Church, they have some level of communion with her and therefore possess elements of salvation within their communities. The obvious implication of the term is that non-Catholic Christians are in "partial communion" with the Catholic Church, although the Church never uses that phrase.

Why not? Maybe because it raises too many questions. Is it actually possible to be in partial communion? Are there different levels of partial communion? Are some levels enough to be saved, while other levels of communion are not? To Catholics before the 1960s, the idea of "partial communion" would have been as non-sensical as a woman being "partially pregnant." And with good reason: the term "communion"—"in union with"—connotes

---

[133] *Unitatis Redintegratio*, 4, emphasis added.

a *total* union. St. Paul writes to the Corinthians, "The cup of blessing which we bless, is it not a communion [*koinōnia*] in the blood of Christ? The bread which we break, is it not a communion [*koinōnia*] in the body of Christ?" (1 Cor. 10:16, modified RSVCE translation). For St. Paul, communion is not something that can be subdivided—one is either in communion with Christ, or not in communion.

Yet the term "full communion" is embraced by both Catholics and non-Catholics as the *raison d'être* for the ecumenical movement. And whereas *Unitatis Redintegratio* spoke of "full communion with the Catholic Church," before long, even Catholics spoke simply of "full communion," without the qualifier, as the goal of ecumenism.

For example, at the end of the council, Pope Paul VI issued a joint declaration with the Orthodox Ecumenical Patriarch, Athenagoras I, that states,

> They [Paul VI and Athenagoras I] hope that the whole Christian world, especially the entire Roman Catholic Church and the Orthodox Church will appreciate this gesture as an expression of a sincere desire shared in common for reconciliation, and as an invitation to follow out in a spirit of trust, esteem and mutual charity the dialogue which, with God's help, will lead to living together again, for the greater good of souls and the coming of the kingdom of God, in that *full communion of faith, fraternal accord and sacramental life* which existed among them during the first thousand years of the life of the Church.[134]

---

[134] *Joint Catholic-Orthodox Declaration of His Holiness Pope Paul VI and the Ecumenical Patriarch Athenagoras*, December 7, 1965, 5, emphasis added.

Note that Paul VI does not reference "full communion with the Catholic Church," but instead simply a "full communion of faith, fraternal accord and sacramental life."

A few years later, the U.S.-based Joint Commission on Anglican-Roman Catholic Relations writes of the goal of their efforts:

> We, the members of the Joint Commission on Anglican-Roman Catholic Relations, now declare that we see the goal as to realize full communion of the Roman Catholic Church with the Episcopal Church and the other Churches of the Anglican Communion.[135]

"Full communion" is apparently the coming together of equal parties; what "full communion" entails is not described.

So what exactly is "full communion"? If it is achieved, what will it look like? These questions reveal the fatal flaw in all ecumenical discussions.

In 2005, the United States Conference of Catholic Bishops (USCCB) releases a document titled "Journey in Faith: Forty Years of Reformed-Catholic Dialogue: 1965-2005,"[136] celebrating four decades of ecumenical dialogues between Catholics and "Reformed" Christians (the term "Reformed" is one that designates Protestant Christians who follow the Calvinist/Presbyterian tradition). The document recounts what each side considers to be "full communion." The Reformed communities define it this way:

---

[135] *ARC VII Statement*, December 1969, https://www.usccb.org/committees/ecumenical-interreligious-affairs/arc-vii-statement.

[136] United States Conference of Catholic Bishops, "Journey in Faith: Forty Years of Reformed-Catholic Dialogue: 1965-2005," 2005, https://www.usccb.org/committees/ecumenical-interreligious-affairs/journey-faith-forty-years-reformed-catholic-dialogue.

When Christians gather at the Lord's Table, they experience unity—a new depth of fellowship with the Lord and with one another—as a gift. They find assurance of reconciliation, forgiveness and healing. They also receive anew the mandate to be part of God's mission, to share the Good News, and to invite all, not least the poor, the weak, the hungry and the oppressed, to join in the banquet.

At the Lord's Table, the church knows itself to be Christ's body, called to present Christ to the world and to do the works of God. In the body of Christ, there is diversity in unity, variety which enriches fellowship, many gifts of the one Spirit (1 Cor. 12:11). Within the body of Christ, love becomes enfleshed in justice and sharing ...

We do not know the precise form of the unity we seek but we believe that it must be such that all in each place must be seen as belonging to one fellowship and that these local, regional or national churches must be in conciliar communion with one another.

Here is how "full communion" is described from the Catholic perspective:

The communion in which Christians believe and for which they hope is, in its deepest reality, their unity with the Father through Christ in the Spirit. Since Pentecost, it has been given and received in the Church, the communion of saints. It is accomplished fully in the glory of heaven, but is already realized in the Church on earth as she journeys toward that fullness. Those who live united 1) in faith, hope and love, 2) in mutual service, 3) in common teaching and sacraments, 4) under the guidance of the pastors are part of that communion which constitutes the Church of God. This communion is realized concretely 5) in the particular churches, each of which is gathered together around its bishop. In each of these "the one, holy, catholic and apostolic Church of Christ is truly present and alive." This communion is, by its very nature, universal.

It is difficult to see any practical unity between these two visions of "full communion." As just one example, although there is mention of "the Lord's Table," the Reformed statement has no concept of a sacramental unity, yet that is essential to a Catholic understanding of "full communion." In spite of the obvious differences, the document goes on to state, "The language may differ in ... the Reformed and the Catholic expressions of the vision. However, the substance is the same." But it simply is not. Saying it is doesn't change what the words mean.

To grasp the essential problem with the language of "full communion," consider this analogy. Two friends are in Kansas, and one says to the other, "Let's go to the best place to live, full of culture and entertainment." The other responds, "Great! I'd love to go to the best place to live, full of culture and entertainment. Let's go!" However, one of the friends believes the best place to live is New York, and the other considers Los Angeles the best place to live. You could say that the "substance" of their understanding of "the best place to live" is the same, yet if they get in a car together to drive there, they will want to go in opposite directions.

In spite of this fundamental issue, "full communion" (without any qualifiers) remains the official stated goal of the Catholic ecumenical movement. In 1995, Pope John Paul II released an encyclical titled *Ut Unum Sint*, "On commitment to Ecumenism," in which he embraces the ambiguous use of the term "full communion." In this document, the phrase "full communion" is used thirty-three times (remember, it was introduced in *Unitatis Redintegratio* yet only used four times in that document). For example, early in the encyclical, the pope writes,

> I myself intend to promote every suitable initiative aimed at making the witness of the entire Catholic community understood in its full purity and consistency, especially considering the engagement which awaits the Church at the threshold of the new Millennium. That will be an exceptional occasion, in view of which she asks the Lord to *increase the unity of all Christians until they reach full communion.*[137]

He then writes that bringing about this full communion is one of his main duties as pope:

> In our ecumenical age, marked by the Second Vatican Council, the mission of the Bishop of Rome is particularly directed to recalling the need for full communion among Christ's disciples.[138]

Now the goal is no longer even full communion with the Catholic Church; it is just "full communion among Christ's disciples." It should go without saying that how a Catholic or an Orthodox or an Anglican or an Evangelical Protestant envisions "full communion among Christ's disciples" will vary widely; yet,

---

[137] *Ut Unum Sint*, 3, emphasis added.
[138] *Ut Unum Sint*, 4.

however ambiguous, this remains the stated goal of the ecumenical movement.

Breeding Indifference

Ecumenism, after being viewed with distaste within Catholic circles for decades, has become one of the most valued tasks of the modern Catholic Church. After getting its official endorsement at Vatican II, Catholic ecumenical work is now seen as an essential mission of the Church. For many Catholic leaders, ecumenism has replaced evangelization as the Church's preeminent form of outreach. Yet the embrace of ecumenism does not come without consequences, and one of the most dire consequences is that ecumenism, at least the modern practice of it, leads to indifference. This happens in three primary ways.

First, the shift that ecumenism requires — from calling non-Catholics to return to the Church to engaging in dialogue with them — gives the impression, if not the downright endorsement, that all parties in ecumenical talks are on equal footing. When it comes to ecumenism, there is no fundamental difference between the two-thousand-year-old Catholic Church founded by Jesus Christ and a nineteenth-century American breakaway sect founded by a religious huckster. Although many (but not all) Catholic ecumenists are careful to insist that they believe the Church of Christ "subsists in" a unique way in the Catholic Church, we've seen that this language nevertheless encourages the idea that the Catholic Church is but one Christian community among many.

Second, and following from the equalizing of all Christian groups, is the assumption that something is "missing" from the Catholic Church, something that will only be fulfilled when the goal of "full communion" is achieved. It is true that many

Catholics, including Church leaders, have committed sins that helped lead to people breaking away from the Church. However, it has always been Church teaching that the Catholic Faith is the *fullness* of the Christian faith; it has no need for additions. Yet ecumenism assumes that something is lacking from Catholicism that can only be fulfilled by non-Catholic Christian communities.

Finally, in official modern ecumenical discussions, there is no misstep more fatal than calling people to convert to another Christian community. As the United States Conference of Catholic Bishops' Executive Director of the Secretariat for Ecumenical and Interreligious Affairs stated, "We Catholics no longer embrace a 'theology of return.' Rather we believe that as all of us seek a deeper conversion to Christ we are coming or will come closer to one another."[139] Since the goal is "full communion," and the definition of "full communion" is disputed, no ecumenist seeks the conversion of those with whom he dialogues. And if there is no call to become Catholic, then many assume there is no need to become Catholic. It has become almost a trope that many Protestant Christians who seek to become Catholic are first told by ecumenically-minded Catholic priests that they don't need to convert. Further, if Church officials do not think it necessary to call non-Catholics to conversion, then it can't be necessary for the average Catholic to encourage the conversion of those around him. And how important can it be even to help

---

[139] John W. Crossin, O.S.F.S., *Ecumenical and Interreligious Sensitivity in Preaching*, https://www.usccb.org/beliefs-and-teachings/ecumenical-and-interreligious/upload/Ecumenical-and-Interreligious-Sensitivity-in-Preaching-Father-John-Crossin.pdf.

one's own children stay Catholic? After all, many paths apparently lead to Heaven. This is the natural consequence of decades of high-ranking Church officials refusing to seek the conversion of their ecumenical dialogue partners.

Ecumenism, first endorsed at Vatican II and then embraced in the decades following the council, has become a breeding ground for religious indifference.

14

Dialogue Supplants Proclamation

Although ecumenism becomes a driving force in the Catholic Church's outreach in the 1960s, it is still only half of the new outreach equation. The other side is interreligious dialogue. The advance of interreligious dialogue takes a similar path to that of ecumenism: hesitant beginnings followed by fevered activity toward a nebulous, ill-defined goal.

Why Interreligious Dialogue?

Interreligious dialogue is slower out of the gate than ecumenism, however, because of course it's far easier to find commonalities between Catholicism and Eastern Orthodoxy, for example, than between Catholicism and Hinduism. Pope Paul VI endorsed interreligious dialogue, but he directed his pontificate more toward ecumenical endeavors. Not until John Paul II does a pope enthusiastically embrace interreligious dialogue and make it a centerpiece of his pontificate. As just one small indicator, in the fifteen years of Paul VI's reign, he made eighty-nine official statements related to interreligious dialogue. In the first fifteen years of John Paul II's reign, he made almost twice as many such statements.[140]

---

[140] Cf. Pontifical Council for Interreligious Dialogue, "Interreligious Dialogue: The Official Teaching of the Catholic Church (1963-1995)."

Ecumenism's goal is "full communion," nebulously defined. What is the goal of interreligious dialogue? This is even more unclear. The original impetus claimed for interreligious dialogue was "peace." After the horrors of two world wars in the first half of the twentieth century, many religious leaders aspired to overcome the barriers of religion, in the hopes that this kind of reconciliation would bring about peace between nations. But over time interreligious dialogue came to be seen as a method to address other worldly problems as well, such as climate change or international refugees. So now at least part of the goal of inter-religious dialogue is working toward the common good.

Beyond this, the goal of interreligious dialogue is often de-scribed with such phrases as "mutual respect," "mutual under-standing," and "mutual conversion." In 1984, the Secretariat for Non-Christians declares that dialogue "means not only discus-sion, but also includes all positive and constructive interreligious relations with individuals and communities of other faiths which are directed at mutual understanding and enrichment."[141] If you're playing interreligious dialogue bingo, you're going to want the word "mutual" on your board.

Catholic participants in interreligious dialogue take pains to emphasize that participants are on equal footing with one an-other and that they are working together to achieve something new and unique. Further, according to the Secretariat for Non-Christians, dialogue is always to be "positive and constructive," which in practice means never criticizing other religious beliefs or practices.

---

[141] Secretariat for Non-Christians, *The Attitude of the Church to-ward Followers of Other Religions: Reflections and Orientations on Dialogue and Mission*, May 10, 1984, 3.

In effect, and perhaps even in intention, this push for mutual respect and mutual understanding results in an equaling of all religions. Whereas Catholics in ages past were urged to avoid attending the religious services of other faiths, Catholics today are urged the opposite. For example, during the COVID-19 pandemic of 2020, when most religious services were moved online, the Diocese of Kansas City-St. Joseph made the following recommendation on its website:

> The Covid-19 pandemic has opened the virtual doors to places of worship that we might not otherwise feel comfortable attending in person. *To grow in mutual respect and understanding,* consider "attending" the below services.[142]

The services listed include a Jewish Shabbat service, many Protestant services, and a Universalist Unitarian service.

Contrast this to the Church's historic interreligious outlook. From her foundations, the Catholic Church has seen other religions and the outside world in general as something to conquer … conquer for Christ. Although there have been eras in which this conquering took on a partially military form, the Church has used persuasion via missionary work as the primary means by which she conquers the world. The mission of the Church is literally to do missions—to convert "the lost" to Christ and His Church. This goal cannot be considered accomplished until the whole world proclaims Christ and everyone is Catholic. Earthly problems were seen as something that would be more

---

[142] July 2020 Pastoral Bulletin, Diocese of Kansas City-St. Joseph, cached version found at https://www.traditioninaction.org/ProgressivistDoc/Internet%20Sources/A_193_KC%20Ecul.pdf, emphasis added.

easily addressed if nations first come to Christ. The priority was the conversion of the nations; the result would be greater peace in the world.

After the 1960s transformation, however, the Church prioritizes solving earthly problems through earthly solutions like dialogue and mutual understanding. Conversion has taken a backseat.

Paul VI Establishes the Model for Dialogue

As the pope who in 1964 established the Secretariat for Non-Christians (later renamed the Pontifical Council on Inter-Religious Dialogue), Pope Paul VI is the papal founder of Catholic interreligious dialogue. He wrote his encyclical *Ecclesiam Suam*, which establishes dialogue as a guiding principle of the Church, that same year. He also presided over Vatican II when it produced *Nostra Aetate*, the official statement of the Church's relations with non-Christian religions.

Paul VI considers interreligious dialogue primarily a means of achieving an earthly (albeit noble) goal: world peace. Speaking to a group of Japanese Buddhists in 1966, he declares,

> We ... call upon all people of religion to play an important role in obtaining a favorable environment in which peace ... can prosper. The Ecumenical Council [Vatican II], which adjourned last year, wished to establish effective contact with all religions, so that an atmosphere of tolerance and mutual respect, with consequent brotherly cooperation and collaboration, could flourish."[143]

[143] Pope Paul VI, *To the Representatives of Japanese Buddhism*, November 7, 1966.

At first the desire for peace is the driving force behind all Catholic interreligious outreach, but over time this singular focus becomes diluted. In 1973, Paul VI declares to the Supreme Buddhist Patriarch of Laos:

> The Catholic Church considers [Buddhism's] spiritual riches with esteem and respect and wishes to collaborate with you, as religious men, to bring about real peace and *the salvation of men.* "Peace" and "salvation" are two ideals that are deeply rooted in the Gospel of Jesus Christ, which we have the mission to proclaim, as also, in some ways, in the Buddhist tradition you follow. They both refer to the Eternal, to the Superterrestrial, and require from man an attitude of detachment, inner freedom, truth, justice and benevolence as the indispensable condition to reach true peace and salvation."[144]

Interreligious dialogue, which originally centered almost solely on fostering world peace, evolves rather quickly into much more, including the explicitly religious yet never well-defined goal of "the salvation of men."

Paul VI also establishes the model for how Church leaders speak of other religions: always positively, never critically. In a 1966 address to the Council of Religions of Vietnam, Paul VI uses the same tone as Vatican II regarding other religions:

> The Catholic Church does not reject anything that is true and good in the various religions. It respects the ways of living and behaving, the doctrines and teachings,

---

[144] Pope Paul VI, *To the Supreme Buddhist Patriarch of Laos*, June 8, 1973, emphasis added.

that indicate the road by means of which men ... seek to reach the stage of perfect illumination with a trusting and humble heart, thanks to their own efforts and the help which comes from above."[145]

Likewise, Paul VI is always positive when speaking of Islam, as in these instances:

We desire to manifest Our esteem for all the followers of Islam living in Africa, who possess elements in common with Christianity from which We enjoy drawing hope for a beneficial dialogue.[146]

We would ... like you to know that the Church recognizes the riches of the Islamic faith — a faith that binds us to the one God.[147]

Further, the language Paul VI uses often puts members of different religions on a level playing field: "All of us are pilgrims to the Absolute and the Eternal, who alone can fulfill the heart of man."[148] Note the "mutual"-type language used: we are all pilgrims, together seeking the same thing, regardless of our religion.

Yet, when speaking to Catholics, Paul VI does affirm that not all religions are equal and that Catholics have a duty to evangelize. In 1973, he states,

[145] Pope Paul VI, *Message to the Council of Religions of Vietnam*, October 5, 1966.

[146] Pope Paul VI, *Message to the Catholic Hierarchy and to All Peoples of Africa*, October 29, 1967.

[147] Pope Paul VI, To the New Ambassador of Pakistan, September 9, 1972.

[148] Pope Paul VI, To the Ven. Gyalwa Karmapa, Buddhist Leader of Tibet, January 17, 1975.

We must admit that not all religious expressions are valid; but we have the good fortune and the duty to affirm that there exists a real religion, subjectively modeled according to the measures and the needs of our spirit, objectively set up by that God whom we are seeking.[149]

And in his apostolic exhortation on evangelization, *Evangelii Nuntiandi*, after affirming his respect and esteem for non-Christian religions, Paul VI writes,

We wish to point out, above all today, that neither respect and esteem for these religions nor the complexity of the questions raised is an invitation to the Church to withhold from these non-Christians the proclamation of Jesus Christ. On the contrary the Church holds that these multitudes have the right to know the riches of the mystery of Christ.[150]

This becomes a confusing model for popes and other Church leaders: acknowledge to Catholics that Catholicism is the true Faith and note that Catholics should evangelize, yet offer only praise and affirmation of other religions when speaking to their adherents. By refusing to publicly critique the beliefs of other religions or to directly call their members to conversion, and by suggesting those religions have a role in the process of salvation, it's understandably difficult for the average Catholic to see what makes Catholicism the true Faith or to discern any urgent reason to call non-Catholics to conversion. For that matter, why should anyone remain Catholic if the going gets tough?

---

[149] Pope Paul VI, To the Faithful in a General Audience, January 31, 1973.

[150] Pope Paul VI, *Evangelii Nuntiandi*, 53.

John Paul II: The Pope of Interreligious Dialogue

If Pope Paul VI established the model for Church leaders when it comes to interreligious dialogue, Pope John Paul II enshrines and expands it. It's hard to overstate how enthusiastically John Paul II embraced interreligious dialogue. During his long pontificate he gave hundreds of addresses to members of other religions — addresses that unanimously affirm the shared values between each of those religions and Catholicism.

Like Paul VI, John Paul II stressed the importance of various religions working together for the common good of the world. To a group of Muslim and Hindu representatives in Kenya, he states,

> The close bonds linking our respective religions — our worship of God and the spiritual values we hold in esteem — motivate us to become *fraternal allies in service* to the human family.[151]

To a group of members of various religions in India, he declares,

> In the world today, there is *a need for all religions to collaborate* in the cause of humanity, and to do this from the viewpoint of the spiritual nature of man. Today, as Hindus, Muslims, Sikhs, Buddhists, Jains, Parsees and Christians, we gather in fraternal love to assert this by our presence.... To work for the attainment and preservation of all human rights ... must become ever more a subject to interreligious collaboration at all levels.[152]

---

[151] Pope John Paul II, *To the Leaders and Representatives of the Islamic and Hindu Communities in Kenya*, August 18, 1985, 3, emphasis in original.

[152] Pope John Paul II, *To the Representatives of the Different Religious and Cultural Traditions in the "Indira Gandhi" Stadium*, February 2, 1986, 7, emphasis in original.

For John Paul II, interreligious dialogue — in which all participating religions are treated as equals — is a vital component in
the quest to build a better world.

In spite of his enthusiastic embrace of interreligious dialogue,
John Paul II acknowledges the key problem, from a Catholic
perspective, with its establishment: How is interreligious dialogue
reconciled with the Church's missionary activity? After all, since
her founding, the Church has gone to all the ends of the earth
not to dialogue with other religions, but to convert people to
Christianity. How then can one promote interreligious dialogue
without abandoning the Church's missionary impulse?

John Paul II addresses this issue directly in his 1990 encyclical *Redemptoris Missio*, whose topic is "the permanent validity
of the Church's missionary mandate." In paragraphs 55-57, the
pope writes of "Dialogue with Our Brothers and Sisters of Other
Religions." He begins by flatly stating, "Inter-religious dialogue is
a part of the Church's evangelizing mission."[153] Yet, based on the
words and actions of John Paul II and other popes, it's difficult
to identify what that part is. Even high-ranking Church leaders
have indicated in the past that dialogue and evangelization are
not compatible. Cardinal Sergio Pignedoli, as the head of the
Secretariat for Non-Christians, said in 1975:

> The Secretariat [for Non-Christians] was certainly not
> created with the intention of proselytizing among non-be-
> lievers, even if that word is understood in a positive sense;
> nor with an apologetic intent but rather with the aim of
> promoting dialogue between believers and unbelievers.[154]

---

[153] Pope John Paul II, *Redemptoris Missio*, 55.
[154] *L'Observatore Romano*, August 21, 1975. Quoted in Romano
Amerio, *Iota Unum* (Kansas City: Sarto House, 1996), 353.

This is the practical result of the embrace of interreligious dialogue by many Catholic leaders: it appears that interreligious dialogue *replaces* the Church's evangelizing mission.

Yet John Paul II insists the two are compatible. After stating that interreligious dialogue is part of evangelization, John Paul II defines interreligious dialogue as a "method and means of mutual knowledge and enrichment." Has the Church ever engaged in this "method and means" in previous generations of missionary work? It is true that Catholic missionaries throughout the ages have at times engaged in the process of inculturation, adapting the Gospel to particular cultures. To do this, it is obviously necessary to know that culture first. Yet, interreligious dialogue, in the modern sense of "mutual enrichment," was unheard of. St. Augustine of Canterbury did not go to the British Isles to gain knowledge of the land and the culture; he went, by order of Pope Gregory the Great, to preach the Gospel. St. Isaac Jogues did not travel to North America for mutual enrichment; he went to save souls by baptizing them. It's unlikely that these great saint-missionaries would have considered interreligious dialogue "part of the Church's evangelizing mission."

For John Paul II, however, interreligious dialogue rests on the belief that the Holy Spirit not only works outside the confines of the Catholic Church, but *through* the practice of other religions. He writes,

> Dialogue does not originate from tactical concerns or self-interest, but is an activity with its own guiding principles, requirements and dignity. It is demanded by deep respect for everything that has been brought about in human beings by *the Spirit who blows where he wills*. Through dialogue, the Church seeks to uncover the "seeds of the

Word," a "ray of that truth which enlightens all men"; these are found in individuals and *in the religious traditions of mankind.*[155]

So, for John Paul II, dialogue unlocks the already-existing Spirit within other religious traditions. And as we've seen, this is a *mutual* process:

> Those engaged in this dialogue must be consistent with their own religious traditions and convictions, and be open to understanding those of the other party without pretense or close-mindedness, but with truth, humility and frankness, knowing that dialogue can enrich each side. There must be no abandonment of principles nor false irenicism, but instead a witness given and received for *mutual advancement* on the road of religious inquiry and experience, and at the same time for the elimination of prejudice, intolerance and misunderstandings.[156]

The implicit equalization of all religions is evident here. In the process of dialogue, Catholics are no different than practitioners of other religions; all participants in interreligious dialogue are on the same path of "mutual advancement." Catholics are to walk side-by-side with non-Catholics on the "road of religious inquiry and experience"; not engage with them to give them the life-giving truth of the Catholic Faith. In the next chapter, we'll find that John Paul II concretizes this equaling of religions in his infamous 1986 World Day of Prayer for Peace in Assisi, Italy.

[155] Pope John Paul II, *Redemptoris Missio*, 56, emphasis added.
[156] Pope John Paul II, *Redemptoris Missio*, 56, emphasis added.

An Ambiguous Mission

In spite of John Paul II's insistence that interreligious dialogue is part of the Church's missionary mandate, it's hard to ignore the fact that the rise to prominence of interreligious dialogue has corresponded with the collapse of missionary activity. The pope himself recognizes this dilemma at the beginning of *Redemptoris Missio* when he muses, "Some people wonder: *Is missionary work among non-Christians still relevant? Has it not been replaced by inter-religious dialogue?*"[157]

Then, the year following *Redemptoris Missio*'s release, the Pontifical Council for Inter-Religious Dialogue issues the document *Dialogue and Proclamation*, addressing the clear tension between interreligious dialogue and the Church's missionary mandate to proclaim the Gospel of Jesus Christ. The document asks questions similar to those of John Paul II: "If interreligious dialogue has become so important, has the proclamation of the Gospel message lost its urgency? Has the effort to bring people into the community of the Church become secondary or even superfluous?"[158]

Both John Paul II and the Pontifical Council for Inter-Religious Dialogue answer these questions in the negative, yet the fact that such questions are continually addressed suggests that the answers given are ultimately unfulfilling. *Dialogue and Proclamation* says of other religions that "they command our respect because over the centuries they have borne witness to the efforts to find answers 'to those profound mysteries of the human condition' (*Nostra Aetate* 1) and have given expression

---

[157] Pope John Paul II, *Redemptoris Missio*, 4.
[158] Pontifical Council for Inter-Religious Dialogue, *Dialogue and Proclamation*, 4.

to the religious experience and they continue to do so today."[159] Later the document states, "the Council [Vatican II] has openly acknowledged the presence of positive values not only in the religious life of individual believers of other religious traditions, but also in the religious traditions to which they belong. It attributed these values to the active presence of God through his Word, pointing also to the universal action of the Spirit,"[160] and "there needs to be mentioned the active presence of the Holy Spirit in the religious life of the members of the other religious traditions."[161] In other words, non-Christian religions deserve the respect of Catholics, because the Holy Spirit works within them.

If this is the case — that the Holy Spirit is active not only in non-Christians, but through the practice of non-Christian religions, then why should Catholics call others to join the Church? And if Mormonism, Judaism, or Buddhism seems appealing, why not switch? *Dialogue and Proclamation* first answers these questions by stating that Jesus mandated proclamation.[162] But then the document notes that even proclamation should be "dialogical, for in proclamation the hearer of the Word is not expected to be a passive receiver. There is progress from the 'seeds of the Word' already present in the hearer to the full mystery of salvation in Jesus Christ. The Church must recognize a process of purification and enlightenment in which the Spirit of God opens the mind and heart of the hearer to the obedience of faith."[163] *Dialogue and Proclamation* is saying

---

[159] *Dialogue and Proclamation*, 14.
[160] *Dialogue and Proclamation*, 17.
[161] *Dialogue and Proclamation*, 28.
[162] See *Dialogue and Proclamation*, 55, 66.
[163] *Dialogue and Proclamation*, 70.

that when a Catholic proclaims the Gospel, he is *still* engaged in dialogue. The Catholic is simply bringing to fulfillment the receiver's already-existing religious beliefs. It sounds as if there is no need for a non-Christian to reject his existing beliefs, doesn't it?

The Emphasis Shift reached its fruition in the pontificate of John Paul II. Far from rejecting false religions and proclaiming Jesus and His Church as the only way to salvation, we must now dialogue with other religions by emphasizing their positive elements. We see this new focus not only in Church documents but in the actions of the pope himself. John Paul II traveled the world and addressed practitioners of many other religions, but his statements and actions when doing so always fit the new dialogue mold—not the historic proclamation model. His example profoundly impacted the beliefs of a generation of Catholics regarding missionary work. Traditionally, saving souls via Baptism was what inspired certain Catholics to leave home and family and to suffer hardships—and the others to support them. Once the goal was morphed into mutual understanding and mutual advancement, however, most Catholics didn't see the point.

The mission of the Church, which has always found its roots in Christ's final words to his disciples to "make disciples of all nations, baptizing them in the name of the Father and of the Son and of the Holy Spirit, teaching them to observe all that I have commanded you" (Matt. 28:19-20), has been made ambiguous. Not only has the Church's interreligious outlook been reduced to finding the positive elements of other religions, the goal has shifted as well: in 1984, the Secretariat for Non-Christians stated that the Church's mission "is also to work for the extension of the kingdom and its values among all men and women."[164] In other words, earthly goals such as world peace, which can be pursued by any secular agency, are now an integral part of the *mission* of the Church. And in practice, these earthly pursuits have become the *primary* part of that mission. Instead of looking to convert the non-Christian world, the Church now works with the non-Christian world to achieve this-worldly goals.

Interreligious dialogue was announced as a duty for the Church in the 1960s under Pope Paul VI, but it became entrenched as an essential part of the Church's outward-facing work during the pontificate of John Paul II. Before we move on to see how this has impacted the Church and her mission after the Polish pope's reign ended, we need to look in more detail at the one event that defined and encapsulated John Paul II's views on interreligious outreach: the 1986 World Day of Prayer for Peace in Assisi, Italy.

[164] Secretariat for Non-Christians, *The Attitude of the Church toward Followers of Other Religions: Reflections and Orientations on Dialogue and Mission*, May 10, 1984, 11.

15

Being Together to Pray:
The Assisi World Day of Prayer

On January 25, 1986, Pope John Paul II makes an announcement at the end of the Week of Christian Unity that startles the Roman Curia: he will hold a "special prayer meeting for peace in the town of Assisi" and this meeting will be "with representatives not only from the various Christian churches and communions but also from other religions across the world."[165]

The event is literally unprecedented; never before has a pope publicly gathered together members of non-Christian religions to pray. In fact, less than 100 years previously, John Paul II's predecessor, Pope Leo XIII, unequivocally opposed a similar meeting held in Chicago in 1893 called the "Parliament of the World's Religions."[166] The meeting in Assisi will become the crowning moment of the Emphasis Shift. It also becomes a symbol of the growing Religious Pluralism and religious indifference within the Church.

The World Day of Prayer for Peace is held on October 27, 1986. The next day the *New York Times* runs the headline, "12

---

[165] Pope John Paul II, *To the Faithful at the Conclusion of the Octave of Prayer for the Unity of Christians*, January 25, 1986.

[166] Cf. Schneider, *Christus Vincit*, 99.

Faiths Join Pope to Pray for Peace." Here are a few excerpts from the article:

> Spiritual leaders from 12 different religions gathered here today to offer individual prayers alongside Pope John Paul II, who had asked them to join him in a "World Day of Prayer for Peace."
>
> The "religious families" represented at the shrine here were African animists; Amerindian animists; Bahais, whose faith stresses universal brotherhood; Buddhists; Christians; Jains, whose beliefs resemble Buddhism; Jews; Hindus; Moslems; Shintoists, a Japanese sect that emphasizes the worship of nature and ancestors; Sikhs, who profess a monotheistic derivation of Hinduism; and Zoroastrians, who believe in the continuous struggle of good against evil.
>
> The religious leaders, who represented every major form of worship, were told by the Pope, "For the first time in history we have come together from everywhere."
>
> The Pope, conspicuous in his all-white cassock, sat with all of the non-Christians in a brightly colored array of dress to his left while on his right were the Christians in variations of black and purple as well as some simple business suits. Elio Toaff, Rome's Chief Rabbi, was the head of the Jewish delegation and sat at the end of the Christian section.[167]

The event is strictly planned beforehand, with Pope John Paul II insisting that the various representatives are not "praying

---

[167] Roberto Suro, "12 Faiths Join Pope to Pray for Peace," *New York Times*, October 28, 1986, sect. A, p. 3.

together," but are "being together in order to pray."[168] Each "religious family" first goes to separate locations around Assisi to pray.
Later they gather together outside the Basilica of St. Francis, and
each pray in turn while the others look on. Photos of the various
religious figures together, with the pope standing out in his white
cassock, appear in newspapers around the globe. Catholics and
non-Catholics understand what a significant event this is in the
history of religions.

John Paul's Motivations

Secular reporters note also the political ramifications of the event;
for example, the *New York Times* reports,

> Guerrilla fighters and warring factions in at least 11 na-
> tions temporarily laid down their weapons in a response
> to the Pope's call for a global 24-hour truce today. The
> Governments of 60 countries, including Israel and Iraq,
> had sent messages supporting the idea, according to the
> chief Vatican spokesman, Joaquin Navarro-Valls, who
> termed the truce initiative "a substantial success."[169]

The pope, however, from the beginning insists that this is an
"event of a religious character, exclusively religious."[170] He sees
prayer as the ultimate means to achieve world peace:

> At Assisi, in an extraordinary way, there was the discov-
> ery of the unique value that prayer has for peace; indeed,

---

[168] Pope John Paul II, *To the Faithful in General Audience*, October
22, 1986, 4.

[169] Suro, "12 Faiths Join Pope to Pray for Peace."

[170] Pope John Paul II, *To the Faithful in General Audience*, October
22, 1986, 1.

it was seen that it is impossible to have peace without prayer, the prayer of all, each one in his own identity and in search of the truth ... Every authentic prayer is under the influence of the Spirit "who intercedes insistently for us." ... We can indeed maintain that every authentic prayer is called forth by the Holy Spirit, who is mysteriously present in the heart of every person.[171]

As a Moderate Inclusivist, John Paul II does not see other religions as strictly "false religions," but he believes that almost every religion contains "seeds of the Word." This means that all religions are in some way a preparation for the Gospel; when properly practiced, they lead to a full flowering of the Gospel. Yes, other religions contain false elements but also truthful seeds within them that can lead people to Christ. And one of the main "seeds" that all religions share is prayer. Speaking before the Assisi meeting, the pope notes,

These are precisely the "traces" or the "seeds" of the Word and the "rays" of the truth. Among these there is undoubtedly prayer.... We respect this prayer even though we do not intend to make our own those formulas that express other views of faith. Nor would the others, on their part, wish to adopt our prayers.[172]

Therefore, if all religions share the "seed" of prayer, then according to John Paul II, it's reasonable for these religions to gather together to pray for a common cause. The only significant difference between the prayers of a Catholic and the prayers of a Buddhist, according to the words of the pope, is that they are

[171] Pope John Paul II, *To the Roman Curia*, December 22, 1986, 11.
[172] Pope John Paul II, *To the Faithful in General Audience*, October 22, 1986, 4.

different "formulations." Yet historically Christians have held that prayers to false gods are of no value and, in fact, are harmful. The pope's statement that non-Catholics do not "wish to adopt our [i.e., Catholic] prayers" implies that Catholics should not encourage them to do so, either.

Along with attributing "seeds of the Word" to other religions, John Paul II also stresses that the Holy Spirit himself works through these other religions. In *Redemptoris Missio*, he writes about the Assisi meeting as an activity of the Holy Spirit:

> Thus the Spirit, who "blows where he wills" (cf. Jn 3:8), who "was already at work in the world before Christ was glorified," and who "has filled the world,...holds all things together [and] knows what is said" (Wis 1:7), leads us to broaden our vision in order to ponder his activity in every time and place. I have repeatedly called this fact to mind, and it has guided me in my meetings with a wide variety of peoples. The Church's relationship with other religions is dictated by a twofold respect: "Respect for man in his quest for answers to the deepest questions of his life, and respect for the action of the Spirit in man." Excluding any mistaken interpretation, the interreligious meeting held in Assisi was meant to confirm my conviction that "every authentic prayer is prompted by the Holy Spirit, who is mysteriously present in every human heart."[173]

For John Paul, then, the Assisi meeting was an opportunity to allow the Holy Spirit to work through the prayers not only of Catholics, but of non-Catholic Christians and even non-Christians. So, according to the pope, the prayers of a polytheistic

---

[173] Pope John Paul II, *Redemptoris Missio*, 29.

Shintoist directed to one of the more than eight million "kami" (the Shinto term for their deities) advances the cause of peace in the world. Further, that prayer is even prompted by the Holy Spirit, as long as it is "authentic."

John Paul also understood the Assisi prayer meeting as the logical result of Vatican II's endorsement of the Emphasis Shift. Speaking to the Roman curia a few months after Assisi, he notes that both *Unitatis Redintegratio* and *Nostra Aetate* formed the foundation of his call for the gathering:

> The source of inspiration ... is always the mystery of unity, both the unity already attained in Christ through faith and Baptism and the unity which is expressed in the condition of being "orientated" toward the People of God and hence is still to be attained perfectly. Thus, as the first unity finds its adequate expression in the Decree *Unitatis Redintegratio* on ecumenism ... the second unity is formulated, on the level of interreligious relationships and dialogue, in the Declaration *Nostra Aetate*.... It is within this second dimension ... that the day of prayer at Assisi offers us precious elements for our reflection, elements that are illuminated by an attentive reading of this declaration on non-Christian religions.[174]

The Emphasis Shift is made flesh in the 1986 World Day of Prayer for Peace held in Assisi.

The Response

Within the halls of diocesan chanceries and parish rectories at the time, the Assisi meeting presents no controversy. The vast

[174] Pope John Paul II, *To the Roman Curia*, December 22, 1986, 8.

majority of Church leaders, who were either part of the Emphasis Shift or were formed after it, are Inclusivists (or Pluralists). Thus, they see Assisi as Pope John Paul II does: a work of the Holy Spirit and a recognition of the elements of truth found in other religions. They do not consider it an embrace of false religions. However, among the small number of Exclusivists, the Assisi meeting is highly controversial. They feel that it is an endorsement of Religious Pluralism by the hierarchy and that it will lead to indifference in the pews.

Pope Leo XIII's opposition to the similar meeting that took place in Chicago in 1893 was diplomatic but clear:

> We have known that meetings are held, from time to time, in the United States, at which Catholics and dissenters from the Catholic Church assemble to discuss together religion and right morals. We, indeed, recognize in this a zeal for religion, by which that nation is daily more ardently moved. Now, although those general meetings have been tolerated by a prudent silence to this day, it would seem, nevertheless, more advisable for Catholics to hold their assemblies apart.[175]

Leo XIII expressed the standard view of most Church leaders until the Emphasis Shift. By 1986 few Catholic leaders or theologians still hold that view, but those who do argue two points. First, Assisi sends a confusing message to the faithful and can lead them astray. Does "being together to pray" mean that all prayers, no matter who (or what) they are directed to, are equal?

---

[175] James F. Cleary, "Catholic Participation in the World's Parliament of Religions, Chicago, 1893," *Catholic Historical Review* 55, no. 4 (1970): 605.

Does this make all religions equal? And the second, more serious, charge: Does an event like Assisi violate the first commandment? That commandment states, "I am the LORD your God. You shall worship the Lord your God and Him only shall you serve." This is the first, and most important, commandment. Critics of the Assisi meeting accuse Pope John Paul II of *de facto*, if not *de jure*, encouragement of the worship of false gods and thus public endorsement of violating the most fundamental commandment.

One event during the Assisi meeting gives credence to both these criticisms. During the time set aside for each religious family to pray separately, the group of Buddhists, led by the Dalai Lama, "quickly converted the altar of the Church of San Pietro by placing a small statue of the Buddha *atop the tabernacle* and setting prayer scrolls and incense burners around it."[176] For Catholics, the tabernacle is the holiest part of a church, for it holds the Holy Eucharist: the Body, Blood, Soul, and Divinity of Jesus Christ. Yet at the Assisi meeting, it is crowned with what Catholics historically consider a false idol for the purpose of public veneration.

At the time of the event, the strongest condemnation came from Archbishop Marcel Lefebvre, founder of the traditionalist Society of St. Pius X. In a joint declaration with fellow traditionalist Bishop Antônio de Castro Mayer, he writes, "The public sin against the one, true God, against the Incarnate Word, and His Church, makes us shudder with horror. John Paul II encourages the false religions to pray to their false gods—an immeasurable, unprecedented scandal."[177] Note the two-fold criticism: the pope encourages the violation of the first commandment, and this

---

[176] Suro, "12 Faiths Join Pope to Pray for Peace," emphasis added.
[177] Marcel Lefebvre and Antônio de Castro Mayer, *Joint Declaration Against Assisi*, December 2, 1986.

leads to great scandal, i.e., an increase of confusion among the faithful as to what is the true religion.

Critics also judge the Assisi meeting to run counter to the practical advice given by St. Paul to the Corinthian church:

> Do not be mismated with unbelievers. For what partnership have righteousness and iniquity? Or what fellowship has light with darkness? What accord has Christ with Belial? Or what has a believer in common with an unbeliever? What agreement has the temple of God with idols? (2 Cor. 6:14-16)

Critics note that even the *appearance* of supporting a false religion is something to be assiduously avoided, particularly by the pope. In the Second Book of Maccabees, Eleazar is an elderly scribe who refuses to eat pork during a persecution initiated by a pagan leader Antiochus IV Epiphanes. As he is led to the rack to be killed, some of his executioners urge him to save himself by eating other meat disguised as pork, thus pretending to follow Antiochus's rule without actually breaking his own religion's rules. But Eleazar refuses, saying, "Such pretense is not worthy of our time of life ... lest many of the young should suppose that Eleazar in his ninetieth year has gone over to an alien religion, and through my pretense, for the sake of living a brief moment longer, they should be led astray because of me, while I defile and disgrace my old age" (2 Macc. 6:24-25). In other words, Eleazar isn't even willing to *pretend* to support another religion, even to save his own life. Yet at Assisi John Paul II gives explicit and public support to the practice of other religions.

As was his habit, the pope refrained from inviting the Assisi participants to convert to Catholicism. He did not evangelize them directly. A few days before the event, in an audience with the Catholic faithful, the pope described the Church's "essential vocation to announce to the world the true salvation which is found only in Jesus Christ, God and man."[178] That was a Wednesday. Then on the following Monday he's with some of the very people who need this announcement and he does not proclaim it. Instead, he notes only that "peace bears the name of Jesus Christ."[179]

The Impact of Assisi

It's hard to overstate the long-term impact of the Assisi prayer meeting. Following the conclusion of the Second Vatican Council, interactions between Catholics and non-Christians expanded and grew more friendly. Yet, never had an interreligious prayer meeting been endorsed, let alone conducted, by a pope. Assisi sends a powerful message to both Catholics and non-Catholics alike that the Emphasis Shift is not simply idle words. The Catholic Church is committed to interreligious dialogue. She is committed to affirming other religions in their own religious practices.

This event announces to the world that Church leaders put Catholicism on an equal footing with other religions, at least when it comes to dealing with world problems. As Vatican observer John Allen wrote thirty years after the event, "The setting in Assisi rather than Rome was deliberate. Rome is the pope's town, while Assisi belongs to St. Francis, a universally admired figure for his commitment to peace, dialogue and simplicity. It was a way of leveling the playing field, making it clear the pope

[178] Pope John Paul II, *To the Faithful in General Audience*, October 22, 1986, 2.
[179] Pope John Paul II, *To Representatives of the Christian Churches and Ecclesial Communities and of the World Religions*, October 27, 1986, 4.

came as a brother to other religions and not a commander-in-chief."[180] Although John Paul might consider this imagery appropriate for addressing world affairs as a united body, to many reasonable people it signaled that all religions are equally valid.

Assisi propelled the increase in Religious Pluralism and thus indifference among Catholics. Although Pope John Paul II was *not* a religious Pluralist, his nuanced views regarding "seeds of the Word" and "being together to pray" are mostly lost on the average Catholic. What most people see is various religious leaders, all equal in standing, praying together for peace. As any political campaigner will tell you, optics are everything, and the optics of this event sent a clear message. The *New York Times* article, after all, declared "12 Faiths Join Pope to Pray for Peace"—not that they gathered separately, but that they "joined" the pope. For most people, the "being together to pray" and "praying together" is a meaningless distinction. Photos that accompany articles around the globe show Pope John Paul II standing alongside other religious leaders ... just one religious leader among many. Regardless of the careful distinctions that existed in the pope's mind, or his intentions, the message received by many is that all religions are equal. And if they are equal, then one can be indifferent to what religion others belong.

Unfortunately, confusion and scandal are the legacy of Assisi. It is indisputable that Pope John Paul II had noble intentions in calling for this gathering. He truly believed that prayer was the best weapon for fostering peace in the world and that the

---

[180] John Allen, "Pope's Inter-Faith Summit in Assisi Belongs to an Ongoing Revolution," *Crux*, September 15, 2016, https://cruxnow.com/analysis/2016/09/popes-inter-faith-summit-assisi-belongs-ongoing-revolution/.

prayers of non-Catholics, even non-Christians, are helpful in that cause. He also felt that bringing together representatives of many religions would help advance toleration between disparate groups. Yet the message received by the world, and by Catholics in the pews, was that any prayer—to anyone or anything—is as good as any other. Further, that any *religion* is as good as any other. Assisi represents a clear message of Religious Pluralism, even if its architect didn't intend it. And considering the rise of Pluralism among Catholics since then, we know that message has been received loud and clear.

16

Throwing Caution to the Wind

Pope John Paul II towers as the most influential Catholic figure of the last quarter of the twentieth century. His views on almost every topic shaped Catholic opinion, including the Church's ecumenism and interreligious outreach. As a Moderate Inclusivist, John Paul had a positive outlook on other religions and encouraged Catholics to share his vision. Although the pope believed that Christ was the only way to salvation, he also emphasized that other religions contained "seeds of the Word" and were often "preparations" for the Gospel. Influenced by his ecumenical and interreligious activities, especially his 1986 prayer meeting at Assisi, Catholics became more and more accepting of non-Christian religions during his reign. John Paul solidified the Church's Emphasis Shift and pushed Catholics further along the Salvation Spectrum toward a more hopeful view of salvation for members of other religions.

After John Paul II, the second-most monumental figure in the Church during the last quarter of the twentieth century and into the beginning of the twenty-first was Joseph Cardinal Ratzinger, the head of the Congregation for the Doctrine of the Faith under Pope John Paul II who would succeed John Paul to the papacy as Benedict XVI. Ratzinger, however, was a Reserved Inclusivist, much less enthusiastic about emphasizing the positive elements of other religions, although he nevertheless largely embraced the Church's Emphasis Shift.

The dangers of relativism deeply concern Joseph Ratzinger; shortly before he is elected pope, he decries the "dictatorship of relativism" plaguing the world and the Church.[181] He opposes the increasingly popular belief that "all religions are equally valid ways of salvation for their followers."[182] He sees dialogue as a way to discover the truth, not just an "exchange of positions that are fundamentally equal and therefore relative to one another."[183]

Yet, both as a high-ranking Vatican official and as pope, he does not oppose ecumenical and interreligious dialogues, and, in fact, he supports and even engages in them himself. Some of his views may confuse observers and even seem contradictory. On the one hand, he decries relativism, but on the other, he supports activities that uphold a relativistic view of religion.

As we've witnessed in the Salvation Spectrum (see chapter 9), the differences along the spectrum are often related more to attitude than theology. Cardinal Ratzinger's *theology* is similar to Pope John Paul II's—they are both Inclusivists—but he has a more cautious *attitude* when it comes to the benefits of ecumenism and interreligious dialogue. His more reserved outlook, however, is resisted by Church leaders and Catholics in the pews; the Emphasis Shift is too well established, and Ratzinger's caution is thrown aside as a remnant of an earlier, darker time. Ratzinger's

---

[181] *Homily of His Eminence Cardinal Joseph Ratzinger*, April 18, 2005.

[182] Joseph Cardinal Ratzinger, *Context and meaning of the "Dominus Iesus" Declaration*, September 5, 2000.

[183] Ratzinger, *Context and meaning of "Dominus Iesus."*

reservations turn out to be no match for the steamroller that is the Emphasis Shift. Two of the more controversial events of his lifetime, the publication of *Dominus Iesus* and his infamous Regensburg Address, illustrate this fact.

Dominus Iesus and the Attempt to Slow the Shift

To get a sense of how Catholics' views of other religions had progressed by the turn of the century, we can take a look at the reaction to an important document released in 2000 by Joseph Cardinal Ratzinger as head of the Congregation for the Doctrine of the Faith. Titled *Dominus Iesus*, its topic is "On the Unicity and Salvific Universality of Jesus Christ and the Church." The document proposes to address the role of Jesus Christ, the Church, and other religions in relation to salvation. *Dominus Iesus* embraces Reserved Inclusivism; if written before 1960, it likely would have been criticized for being too optimistic about the salvation of non-Catholics, but coming out forty years into the Emphasis Shift, it attracted fierce criticism within the Church for not being optimistic *enough*. So the reaction to it demonstrates how far along the Salvation Spectrum most of the Church had traveled in four decades.

Dominus Iesus was released in response to the increase in the number of Catholic theologians arguing that there are other ways to salvation, apart from Jesus Christ and His Church. Compared to most Church documents written after the Emphasis Shift, *Dominus Iesus* is much more definitive in its statements on the necessity of the Catholic Church for salvation. Early in the document the CDF explicitly expresses concern about the rise of Pluralism: "The Church's constant missionary proclamation is endangered today by relativistic theories which seek to justify religious pluralism, not only *de facto* but also *de iure (or in principle)."*[184] We know that Religious Pluralism was gaining a foothold among theologians. Pluralism among Catholics was flourishing particularly in Asia, where they were a minority and in regular contact with adherents of many different non-Christian religions. But instead of questioning whether the Church's practice of interreligious dialogue contributes to the rise of Religious Pluralism, *Dominus Iesus* stubbornly argues that dialogue is an essential part of proclamation. The document rightly affirms the Church's official teaching of *extra ecclesiam nulla salus*. However, in the next breath it continues to defend (and explain) the Vatican II phrase "subsists in," which we've seen weakened practical support for the doctrine of EENS.

Near the end of the document, after stating the official teaching that the Church is necessary for salvation, *Dominus Iesus* includes what has become standard since the Emphasis Shift: a reassurance that non-Christians can be saved, as well as praise for other religions and their religious practices:

> With respect to the way in which the salvific grace of God—which is always given by means of Christ in the Spirit and has a mysterious relationship to the Church—comes to individual non-Christians, the Second Vatican Council limited itself to the statement that God bestows it "in ways known to himself." Theologians are seeking to understand this question more fully. Their work is to be encouraged, since it is certainly useful for understanding better God's salvific plan and the ways in which it is accomplished....
>
> Certainly, the *various religious traditions contain and offer religious elements which come from God, and which*

[184] Congregation for the Doctrine of the Faith, *Dominus Iesus*, 4.

are part of what "the Spirit brings about in human hearts and in the history of peoples, in cultures, and religions." Indeed, *some prayers and rituals of the other religions may assume a role of preparation for the Gospel,* in that they are occasions or pedagogical helps in which the human heart is prompted to be open to the action of God.[185]

In spite of the fact that *Dominus Iesus* is truly an Inclusivist document, its reserved nature toward the value of other religions leads to significant backlash among many Catholic theologians and even bishops, reflecting the Church's move further and further along the Salvation Spectrum toward Pluralism. Reserved Inclusivism is not enough anymore; an Expansive Inclusivism, or even Religious Pluralism, is now necessary.

We find a similar process in the modern political world. In general, liberals push the envelope of what is acceptable, while conservatives try to hold on to previous norms and beliefs. In recent decades, liberals have gained a lot of ground in the cultural landscape. Eventually, as what used to be debatably immoral becomes accepted behavior, conservatives find themselves supporting what were liberal causes ten years previously (while liberals have moved on to the next battle). For instance, decades ago contraception was illegal. At the time of its legalization, conservatives opposed the move. Of course, they eventually accepted it, so liberals moved on to demanding the government and employers pay for it. Can you imagine how crazy a conservative would seem today if he argued that contraception should be illegal? That ground was lost long ago. Returning to *Dominus Iesus,* many in the Church felt that the document sought to reopen

[185] Congregation for the Doctrine of the Faith, *Dominus Iesus*, 21, emphasis added.

a debate that had long been settled. Ratzinger seemed about as retrograde as someone trying to ban the Pill.

After *Dominus Iesus* is released, the *Los Angeles Times* runs an article headlined, "Vatican Declares Catholicism Sole Path to Salvation."[186] This article causes a great deal of consternation among American bishops, and many take pains to argue that *Dominus Iesus* does not, in fact, declare that Catholicism is the sole path to salvation. The Cardinal Archbishop of Los Angeles, Roger Mahony, writes,

> In light of the great progress made in ecumenical and interreligious dialogue in the greater Los Angeles area, it is discouraging to read the headline "Vatican Declares Catholicism Sole Path to Salvation" (*Los Angeles Times*, Sept. 6, 2000). While clarifying the Roman Catholic Church's position, the declaration does in fact affirm that those who are not formally part of the Roman Catholic Church can indeed be saved (*Dominus Iesus*, 20).[187]

The archbishop of Newark, Theodore McCarrick, argues,

> The headlines trumpeted that Catholics think they are the only ones who can be saved, that the pope called other religions inferior and that the Catholic Church was returning to what the media so glibly inferred to have been a past of intolerance and intransigence. What nonsense, especially in the light of our Holy Father's constant

---

[186] Richard Boudreaux and Larry B. Stammer, "Vatican Declares Catholicism Sole Path to Salvation," *Los Angeles Times*, September 6, 2000.

[187] "Dialogues Will Continue," Statement by Cardinal Roger Mahony, Los Angeles, September 9, 2000.

outreach to other faiths and other religious leaders. ... We do not claim that only Catholics can be saved or that only Catholics can be holy.[188]

Pittsburgh bishop Donald Wuerl states flatly, "If that article were a tire, it's so full of defects it would be recalled."[189]

These are not the statements of a few obscure, fringe bishops; Mahony was the Cardinal Archbishop of the largest diocese in America, and Wuerl and McCarrick would later be appointed Cardinal Archbishops of Washington, DC in succession (Mc-Carrick just two months later in November 2000, and Wuerl in 2006).

Yet the *Los Angeles Times* headline is factually correct: *Dominus Iesus* does claim that Catholicism is the sole path to salvation, although that is not the same thing as saying that only Catholics can be saved. Mahoney, McCarrick, Wuerl and others, however, are not interested in affirming the necessity of the Church for salvation; they are much more concerned with asserting that many (most?) people can be saved without formal membership in the Church. Instead of affirming the ordinary path to salvation, they trip over each other to point out the extraordinary means of salvation.

The American bishops, along with bishops and theologians around the world, are mostly concerned with the *tone* of the document. Fr. Peter Chirico, writing in the influential Jesuit periodical *America*, sums up nicely a primary criticism of *Dominus*

---

[188] "Ways of Misunderstanding This Document," Statement by Archbishop Theodore McCarrick, Newark, New Jersey, September 12, 2000.

[189] Ann Rodgers-Melnick, "Wuerl: Others Can Be Saved," *Pittsburgh Post-Gazette*, September 7, 2000.

Iesus: "I … believe that the document was written the way it would have been written 60 years ago."[190] Of course, this criticism ignores the fact that *Dominus Iesus* makes statements about other religions that would never have been included in Church documents before the 1960s. Even so, *Dominus Iesus* seems like a step backward. This reflects the reality in the pews at the time: Religious Pluralism, or at least Expansive Inclusivism, was so implicitly accepted among Catholics that even *Dominus Iesus'* Reserved Inclusivism looked retrograde by comparison. The reaction to *Dominus Iesus* by Church leaders only affirms for the average Catholic that belief in the Church as the unique means to salvation is no longer required.

The Regensburg Address

By the time of *Dominus Iesus'* release in 2000, the Church had traveled far along the Salvation Spectrum. Effectively, most Church leaders at this time, and the majority of Catholics, were at the very least Expansive Inclusivists, if not religious Pluralists. The reaction to another Ratzinger event just a few years later (and after Ratzinger was elected pope) further illuminates the path to Pluralism within the Church.

In September 2006, Pope Benedict XVI addresses the faculty at the University of Regensburg in Germany. He discusses the relationship between faith and reason, and during his address he quotes the fourteenth-century Byzantine Emperor Manuel II who said, "Show me just what Muhammad brought that was new and there you will find things only evil and inhuman, such as his command to spread by the sword the faith he

---

[190] Peter Chirico, "Dominus Iesus as an Event," *America*, March 26, 2001.

preached."[191] The pope uses this quote as a starting point for a discussion on the relationship between religion and violence, and he even notes that Manuel II spoke with a "brusqueness that we find unacceptable."

Yet this critique does not prevent a fervent outcry from the Muslim world accusing the pope of endorsing the views of Manuel II. Many Catholics join in this outcry, particularly those involved in interreligious dialogue. They regard it unacceptable for a pope even to suggest something negative about Islam. One Argentinian Cardinal says, "Benedict's statement[s] don't reflect my own opinions. ... These statements will serve to destroy in 20 seconds the careful construction of a relationship with Islam that Pope John Paul II built over the last 20 years."[192] Those words were spoken by Cardinal Jorge Bergoglio, who a few years later would become Pope Francis.

The pushback from both the Islamic and Catholic worlds was so great it forced Pope Benedict to issue an apology:

I am deeply sorry for the reactions in some countries to a few passages of my address at the University of Regensburg, which were considered offensive to the sensibility of Muslims. These in fact were a quotation from a medieval text, which do not in any way express my personal thought. I hope this serves to appease hearts and to clarify the true meaning of my address, which in its totality was

---

[191] Pope Benedict XVI, "Faith, Reason and the University: Memories and Reflections," Aula Magna of the University of Regensburg, September 12, 2006.

[192] Alasdair Baverstock, "Pope Francis' Run-In with Benedict XVI over the Prophet Mohammed," *Daily Telegraph* (London), March 15, 2013.

and is an invitation to frank and sincere dialogue, with mutual respect.[193]

The Emphasis Shift is complete. Even the *suggestion* of criticism of another religion is now *verboten* among Catholics. The party line of the Emphasis Shift looks only at the positive elements of other religions and insists that members of other religions can be saved. Any deviation from this party line, however slight, is harshly silenced, even if that deviation comes from the pope himself.

The Legacy of Ratzinger/Benedict

In his long ecclesial career, Joseph Ratzinger tried to nudge the Church toward Reserved Inclusivism on the Salvation Spectrum. However, he will likely be remembered more for his failure in this regard. And this failure demonstrates the inevitable push toward Pluralism that occurs after the embrace of any degree of Inclusivism, even to a reserved degree.

As pope, Benedict XVI even held his own Assisi World Day of Prayer for Peace — the event most associated in the public eye with Pluralism — at which representatives from many world religions were again brought together to pray for peace. Although the pope did not include a joint interreligious prayer gathering at this event, he never rejected joint prayer gatherings on principle. He only noted that "there are undeniable dangers, and it is indisputable that the Assisi meetings, especially in 1986, were misinterpreted by many people."[194] In other words, there's

---

[193] "Pope Benedict XVI in his own words," *BBC News*, February 11, 2013.

[194] Joseph Cardinal Ratzinger, *Truth and Tolerance* (San Francisco: Ignatius Press, 2004), 107.

nothing inherently wrong with a pope encouraging the prayer of practitioners of other religions; the real danger is that such an action can be "misinterpreted."

The final word on Ratzinger/Benedict's failure to nudge the Church even a little bit in the direction of Reserved Inclusivism is the election of the man to succeed him as pope. In Pope Francis, we find someone who backs the steamrolling process of moving closer and closer to Pluralism on the Salvation Spectrum.

17

Pope Francis Accelerates the Shift

By the time Jorge Bergoglio was elected Supreme Pontiff of the Roman Catholic Church in March 2013, the Emphasis Shift had become institutionalized. Paul VI, John Paul II, and Benedict XVI, all in their own ways, embraced and continued the Emphasis Shift. Pope Francis, for his part, championed this trend with new enthusiasm, embracing the new outlook while putting his own personal touch on it, ultimately pushing Catholics even more toward religious indifference.

"Proselytism Is a Solemn Nonsense"

The Church statements examined show us that, in the years following the Emphasis Shift, Church leaders recognized a tension between the modern call for "dialogue" and the historic duty of "proclamation." The Pontifical Council for Inter-Religious Dialogue even produced a document on this topic in 1991 called *Dialogue and Proclamation*. The tension can be summed up in this question: Is the Church called to proclaim the Gospel to the nations, or is she supposed to dialogue with them? This question gets to the heart of the Church's mission, and how it is answered has deep ramifications for how Catholics view the role of the Church in bringing salvation to themselves and to the world.

Before the Emphasis Shift, the answer was simple: the Church was called to proclaim the Gospel, period. Proclamation was the method by which the Church engaged with the wider world. There was no endorsement of "dialogue" as a method until Pope Paul VI's 1964 encyclical *Ecclesiam Suam*. However, once dialogue replaced proclamation as the standard operating procedure for relating to non-Catholics, advocates for dialogue faced a problem. Simply discarding proclamation like an old relic didn't seem right. Didn't that amount to a rejection of legitimate Catholic tradition? So the challenge arose: how to reconcile the new method of dialogue with the old method of proclamation.

The method of Paul VI, John Paul II, and Benedict XVI for easing this tension was to downplay its significance. Dialogue was declared complementary to proclamation. As the Pontifical Council for Inter-Religious Dialogue put it, "Proclamation and dialogue are thus both viewed, each in its own place, as component elements and authentic forms of the one evangelizing mission of the Church. They are both oriented towards the communication of salvific truth."[195] Nevertheless, in practical terms, dialogue overwhelmed proclamation. Since the 1960s, popes have only publicly engaged in dialogue with non-Catholics, never proclamation to them. Yet all the while Church leaders insist that both dialogue and proclamation are necessary parts of the Church's "evangelizing mission."

Pope Francis is different. He barely gives lip service to proclamation; he downplays or even opposes it. He's engaged in a war against what he considers one of the greatest sins we can commit: *proselytism*.

---

[195] Pontifical Council for Inter-Religious Dialogue, *Dialogue and Proclamation*, 2.

What is proselytism? A dictionary definition is "to induce someone to convert to one's faith," which seems to be a synonym for evangelization. But within the Church, this term has a more negative meaning; it is often seen as the process of *forcing* someone, against his free choice, to convert. This force could be physical or psychological, through manipulative means. Certainly the practice would be considered sinful.

Pope Benedict XVI rejected proselytism as defined in this negative sense, saying, "The Church does not engage in proselytism. Instead, she grows by 'attraction,'"[196] Francis too rejects proselytism and says he endorses evangelization. In a discussion with a group of Jesuits about the difference between two, Francis says, "What I mean is that evangelization is free! Proselytism, on the other hand, makes you lose your freedom."[197] The connection of proselytism with a loss of freedom is the meaning Pope Benedict XVI gave the word, and this is what he condemned: forced conversions, either through physical force or other illicit means of pressure. Francis also condemns situations such as prosperity Gospel preachers promising material success if one converts.

The problem with Francis's statements condemning what he calls proselytism is that he often blurs the line between (legitimate) evangelization and (illegitimate) proselytism. The loss of freedom is an important distinction between the two, but what

---

[196] Pope Benedict XVI, *Holy Mass for the Inauguration of the Fifth General Conference of the Bishops of Latin America and the Caribbean*, May 13, 2007.

[197] Antonio Spadaro, S.J., "Pope's meeting with Jesuits in Mozambique and Madagascar," *Vatican News*, September 5, 2019, https://www.vaticannews.va/en/pope/news/2019-09/pope-conversations-jesuits-mozambique-madagascar-spadaro.html.

constitutes a loss of freedom to Francis is so broad that *any* action to promote conversion, even one that does not include physical or psychological force, is reprehensible.

A few examples illuminate his attitude toward evangelization:

When asked a question by a girl who was interested in bringing her unchurched friends with her to church, the pope replied, "It is not licit that you convince them of your faith; proselytism is the strongest poison against the ecumenical path."[198]

In an interview on the topic of ecumenism: "There is a policy we should have clear in every case: to proselytize in the ecclesial field is a sin.... Proselytism is a sinful attitude. It would be like transforming the Church into an organization. Speaking, praying, working together: this is the path that we must take."[199]

In response to an atheist reporter who said to him, "My friends think it is you [who] want to convert me," Francis replies, "Proselytism is solemn nonsense, it makes no sense. We need to get to know each other, listen to each other and improve our knowledge of the world around us."[200]

[198] Matthew Cullinan Hoffman, "Ecumenism, 'Proselytism', and the Danger of Doctrinal Ambiguity," *Catholic World Report*, December 9, 2016, https://www.catholicworldreport.com/2016/12/09/ecumenism-proselytism-and-the-danger-of-doctrinal-ambiguity/.

[199] David Gibson, "Francis Interview: Excerpts on Ecumenism, Terrorism and Gossip," *National Catholic Reporter*, October 28, 2016, https://www.ncronline.org/news/vatican/francis-interview-excerpts-ecumenism-secularism-terrorism-and-gossip.

[200] Interview with Eugenio Scalfari, "The Pope: How the Church Will Change," *La Repubblica*, October 1, 2013, https://www.

When meeting with a group of Jesuits, Francis was asked for recommendations "so that our evangelization is not proselytism." He answered: "Today I felt a certain bitterness after a meeting with young people. A woman approached me with a young man and a young woman. I was told they were part of a slightly fundamentalist movement. She said to me in perfect Spanish: 'Your Holiness, I am from South Africa. This boy was a Hindu and converted to Catholicism. This girl was Anglican and converted to Catholicism.' But she told me in a triumphant way, as though she was showing off a hunting trophy. I felt uncomfortable and said to her, 'Madam, evangelization yes, proselytism no.'"[201]

Based on these and many other examples, Francis appears to reject any and all attempts to convert another person, no matter the means used. After all, the pope knew nothing about how the Hindu and Anglican converted to Catholicism, yet his initial reaction is to condemn the young woman who introduces them as converts. Further, he tells another young woman, "It is not licit that you convince them of your faith," a clear rejection of *any* attempt to convert non-Catholics, no matter the means. Evangelization, then, is reduced to being a good example by living a good life, with no duty to explicitly invite others to convert (and in fact a duty *against* inviting conversions!).

For Francis, asking a person to convert somehow inherently necessitates a loss of freedom. Instead of trying to convert

repubblica.it/cultura/2013/10/01/news/pope_s_conversation _with_scalfari_english-67643118/.

[201] Antonio Spadaro, S.J., "Pope's Meeting with Jesuits in Mozambique and Madagascar," *Vatican News*, September 5, 2019, https://www.vaticannews.va/en/pope/news/2019-09/pope-conversations-jesuits-mozambique-madagascar-spadaro.html.

non-Catholics, then, Catholics must *only* dialogue with them, getting to know each other and walking along the same path (although where that path leads is an open question).

This attitude completely undercuts any concept of proclamation. Although technically speaking, seeking conversions isn't the same thing as proclaiming the Gospel, what is the purpose of this proclamation if not to convert souls to Catholicism? By showing an almost allergic reaction to conversions to Catholicism, Francis is sidelining the role of proclamation.

While more extreme than anything expressed by other post-Vatican II pontiffs, Francis's attitude is a logical outgrowth of the Church's Emphasis Shift. We went from emphasizing proclamation to emphasizing dialogue. Naturally the end goal first became muddled, then eventually transformed into something completely different. The goal of proclamation is conversion; the goal of dialogue is ... more dialogue?

Discouraging conversions, and thereby handicapping proclamation, leads to greater religious indifference. The driving force behind seeking conversions is a fundamental belief that being Catholic *matters*. If Catholics are not supposed to invite others to become Catholic, then they feel that being Catholic themselves perhaps isn't so important. This gives religious indifference room to fester. And the process is cyclical: as religious indifference grows, Catholics are less motivated to proclaim the Gospel and seek conversions. The pontiff's rejection of conversions builds another layer on the edifice of religious indifference that has been developing since the Emphasis Shift.

A Focus on This World

Even the most casual observer of Francis recognizes that his pontificate is scrupulously concerned with political issues, such as climate change, immigration, and economic systems. Early in his pontificate, the pope said that the "most serious of the evils that afflict the world these days are youth unemployment and the loneliness of the old."[202] Millions of people are leaving the Church, and the overall influence of Catholicism is dramatically waning, but the real problem for Church leaders is out-of-work millennials. The pope's most famous, most promoted, and most well-known writing is his encyclical *Laudato Si'*, which consists mostly of political, not religious, admonitions and opinions. His laser focus on this-worldly goals, however, is a sure path to increased religious indifference.

Improving the world has been the driving force behind the Church's involvement in interreligious dialogue since the time of Pope Paul VI. But for Francis, because improving this world is his primary focus, interreligious dialogue takes center stage in his pontificate. Dialogue is *the* means for achieving peace, according to the pope. In an address to an International Meeting for Peace, he says,

> As leaders of different religions there is much we can do. Peace is the responsibility of everyone. To pray for peace, to work for peace! A religious leader is always a man or woman of peace, for the commandment of peace is inscribed in the depths of the religious traditions that we represent. But what can we do? Your annual meeting suggests the way forward: the courage of dialogue ... Peace requires a persistent, patient, strong, intelligent dialogue by which nothing is lost. Dialogue can overcome war. Dialogue can bring people of different generations who

[202] Scalfari, "How the Church Will Change."

often ignore one another to live together; it makes citizens of different ethnic backgrounds and of different beliefs coexist. Dialogue is the way of peace.[203]

Of course, nothing exemplifies "Dialogue is the way of peace" more than the Assisi World Days of Prayer for Peace, held twice by John Paul II (1986, 2002) and once by Benedict (2011). Pope Francis also holds one in 2016 for the thirtieth anniversary of the first Assisi meeting. Ironically, in his address to the various religious representatives, he deplores the "paganism of indifference." However for Francis the problem was not one of indifference to the distinctions between religions, but indifference toward religion in general, and indifference toward peace. It doesn't matter what religion you are, what matters is your commitment to certain earthly goals.

> God asks this of us, calling us to confront the great sickness of our time: indifference. It is a virus that paralyzes, rendering us lethargic and insensitive, a disease that eats away at the very heart of religious fervour, giving rise to a new and deeply sad paganism: the *paganism of indifference*. We cannot remain indifferent. Today the world has a profound thirst for peace.[204]

Even when Francis writes an apostolic exhortation on evangelization, he emphasizes dialogue and extols its practical benefits for the world:

---

[203] Pope Francis, *Address to Participants in the International Meeting for Peace Sponsored by the Community of Sant'Egidio*, September 30, 2013.

[204] Pope Francis, *Address of the Holy Father*, Assisi, September 20, 2016, emphasis in original.

Evangelization also involves the path of dialogue. For the Church today, three areas of dialogue stand out where she needs to be present in order to promote full human development and to pursue the common good: dialogue with states, dialogue with society — including dialogue with cultures and the sciences — and dialogue with other believers who are not part of the Catholic Church.[205]

Specifically writing about interreligious dialogue, the pontiff notes,

Interreligious dialogue is a necessary condition for peace in the world, and so it is a duty for Christians as well as other religious communities. This dialogue is in first place a conversation about human existence or simply, as the bishops of India have put it, a matter of "being open to them, sharing their joys and sorrows." In this way we learn to accept others and their different ways of living, thinking and speaking. We can then join one another in taking up the duty of serving justice and peace, which should become a basic principle of all our exchanges. A dialogue which seeks social peace and justice is in itself, beyond all merely practical considerations, an ethical commitment which brings about a new social situation.[206]

It might seem odd to critique a pope's efforts to promote peace and the common good in the world. After all, aren't those good things? The problem lies in the means by which it is being done. Historically, the Church understood that true peace

---

[205] Pope Francis, *Evangelii Gaudium*, 238.
[206] Pope Francis, *Evangelii Gaudium*, 250.

only comes through faith in Jesus Christ, the Prince of Peace. By evangelizing others to become Catholic, one is promoting peace. Now, however, the pope is putting the Church on a level playing field with all other religions in a quest for peace. And in fact, we are called to accept other religions as no better or worse than Catholicism. As Pope Francis says, by dialoguing for peace with other religious communities "we learn to accept others and their different ways of living, thinking and speaking." Yet this process of "accepting" the ways of other religions, by its very nature, means not judging them as false or in any way deficient.

Ultimately, by promoting dialogue to resolve political and economic affairs, Francis sends a message that the purpose of religion—all religions—is to help "fix" this world. The differences between the religions are of secondary, if any, concern. What matters most is saving this world, not gaining entrance into the next.

By downplaying conversions to Catholicism and focusing on worldly concerns, Pope Francis accelerates the growing religious indifference within the Church, an indifference that other pontiffs also fostered. Yet Pope Francis did something in 2019 that no other pope before him did: he endorsed in an official capacity the idea of Religious Pluralism. We'll explore this event and its ramifications in the next chapter.

18

"Willed by God": The Abu Dhabi Declaration

If there's one thing I've been trying to make clear in this book, it's that the dramatic changes that have occurred in the Church's ecumenical and interreligious outlook since the 1960s are due more to a *shift in emphasis* than an *explicit change in doctrine*. In Church documents and papal statements, the language used is careful not to cross the line into official theological heresy (though often leading people to religious indifference, nevertheless). Yet in 2019 Pope Francis releases a document that *does* appear to cross that line and, in fact, endorses Religious Pluralism.

Melding Religions

Since the terrorist attacks of September 11, 2001, interreligious dialogue between Catholics and Muslims has explored ways to prevent religiously inspired violence. Many local and national interreligious groups have released joint statements condemning violence and promoting dialogue as a means to peace. In February 2019 the pope himself also releases such a statement, co-authored by prominent Sunni Islamic leader Sheikh Ahmad al-Tayyeb, Grand Imam of Al-Azhar. Titled A *Document on Human Fraternity for World Peace and Living Together*, the text urges "all persons who have faith in God and faith in *human fraternity* to unite and work together so that [this document] may serve as a guide for future generations to advance a culture of mutual respect in the awareness of the great divine grace that makes all human beings brothers and sisters."[207] Signed in Abu Dhabi, the capital of the United Arab Emirates, this statement is often called the "Abu Dhabi Declaration."

In many ways, the Abu Dhabi Declaration is a standard-fare interreligious dialogue statement in keeping with the Emphasis Shift. Pope Francis says, "I openly reaffirm this: from the Catholic point of view the Declaration does not move one millimetre away from the Second Vatican Council,"[208] and while some might say that is an exaggeration, the document does contain typical interreligious dialogue language found in the Vatican II documents and that has been commonly used since the Emphasis Shift. For example, the desire to foster "mutual respect" has been a frequent theme of these statements since the 1960s, and it's front and center in the Abu Dhabi Declaration.

Early on in the declaration, the pope and the sheikh state that "In the name of God ... [we] declare the adoption of a culture of dialogue as the path; mutual cooperation as the code of conduct; reciprocal understanding as the method and standard." Does anything there catch your eye? If the pope and sheikh state together that they write "in the name of God," then they imply that they believe in the same God ... and their God has

---

[207] Pope Francis and Sheikh Ahmad al-Tayyeb, *A Document on Human Fraternity for World Peace and Living Together*, February 4, 2019, emphasis in original. All succeeding quotes from this document will not be footnoted, as there are no paragraph numbers within the text.

[208] Pope Francis, *Press Conference on the Return Flight from Abu Dhabi to Rome*, February 5, 2019.

the same name. Yet Catholics believe that the "name" of God is "the Father, the Son, and the Holy Spirit" (cf. Matt. 28:19); i.e., the Holy Trinity, a teaching that Islam emphatically rejects. Catholics and Muslims making a joint statement "in the name of God" suggests that there is no fundamental difference between the two religions as to the "name" of God.

In addition, the Abu Dhabi Declaration treats "religion" as a single phenomenon. The modern world does indeed lump all religions into a single category: "religion." We see this whenever someone commits a crime in the name of his religion; many pundits then decry the impact of "religion" on the susceptible, without any regard to the specifics of any one religion. Yet the Catholic Church has historically (and understandably) seen Catholicism as the only true religion, with all other religions containing at least some fundamental falsehoods. Yes, some religions share certain beliefs and practices with others, but religions are too fundamentally different to accurately classify them all under one heading. Thus, a single category of "religion" that includes both Catholicism and all other religions does not align with the historic Catholic view of the world.

The Abu Dhabi Declaration states that "among the most important causes of the crises of the modern world" are "a distancing from *religious* values," and then later makes a blanket condemnation of "*religious* extremism." Further, the document goes on to "affirm ... the importance of awakening *religious* awareness" as a means to "confront tendencies that are individualistic, selfish, conflicting, and also address radicalism and blind extremism in all its forms and expressions."

In these statements we see an equalization of religions, a problem that has plagued interreligious dialogue since the beginning. What are "religious values"? Does this mean the values of all religions are the same? If so, how does, for example, the Catholic view of women co-exist as an equal value with the Muslim view of women? What does it mean that "religious extremism" is bad? Does this mean a Catholic "extremist" like Mother Teresa equates with an Islamic extremist like Osama bin Laden? And what is "religious awareness"? If a person becomes "more aware" of the religion of Satanism, is this a way to confront selfish tendencies, as the text suggests? By conflating all religions the pope and the sheikh endorse religious indifference. All religions are equally valuable, so what's the point of preferring one over the other?

What Is Willed by God?

So is the Abu Dhabi Declaration just another in a long line of interreligious dialogue statements produced by Church officials? If what has been mentioned were the only ways the document was problematic, it would not be necessary to single it out in a separate chapter of this book. Sadly, many other interreligious statements contain these errors. However, a specific passage in this document crosses a theological line that no other Church document in the past had crossed and that makes this document singular in nature. That passage states, "The pluralism and the diversity of religions, colour, sex, race and language are willed by God in His wisdom, through which He created human beings." Breaking this sentence down, this document is claiming that the following things are *willed by* God:

* The pluralism and the diversity of religions
* Colour (presumably, this means various skin colors)
* Sex
* Race
* Language

For our purposes, it is that first item on the list which is alarming. The pope is saying that the pluralism of religions is *willed by God*. I'm highlighting the "willed by God" again because it is so important. In fact, that statement is the explicit belief of the religious Pluralist — that the multitude of religions in this world is not a bad thing but, in fact, is willed by God to lead many people to salvation. If God *wills* Protestantism and Hinduism, there is certainly no need to pray or work for the conversion of ... well, anyone at all.

Some of the pope's defenders say that's not what he means. Catholic theology professor Chad Pecknold argues, "In sensitive inter-religious contexts, it is fitting for the Holy See to acknowledge that despite serious theological disagreements, Catholics and Muslims have much in common, such as a common belief that human beings are 'willed by God in his wisdom.'"[209] In other words, it is the beliefs shared by Catholics and Muslims that is willed by God, not the errors of Islam or other religions. That's quite a stretch from a plain reading of the text.

Pecknold also notes, "God wills that all men come to know Him through the free choice of their will, and so it follows that a diversity of religions can be spoken about as *permissively willed* by God without denying the supernatural good of one true religion."[210] Let's take a look at this phrase "permissively willed," because Pecknold's defense of this aspect of the Abu Dhabi Declaration is important.

---

[209] Mary Farrow, "Pope Francis Signs Peace Declaration on 'Human Fraternity' with Grand Imam," *Catholic News Agency*, February 4, 2019, https://www.catholicnewsagency.com/news/pope-francis-signs-peace-declaration-on-human-fraternity-with-grand-imam-98253.

[210] Farrow, "Pope Francis Signs Peace Declaration," emphasis added.

Catholic theologians have historically distinguished between the "active" will of God and His "permissive" will. What God actively wills is what He *wants* to happen, such as the salvation of all people (cf. 1 Tim. 2:4). On the other hand, what God permissively wills are things that He *allows* to happen. This is the short answer to the age-old question, "If God is all-powerful, why is there evil in the world?" It's not that God cannot prevent evil; instead, He allows it in His permissive will so that a greater good can be accomplished. So, based on this understanding, Pecknold and others are arguing that in the Abu Dhabi document the pope actually means that the plurality of religions is *permissively* willed by God, not *actively* willed.

However, many others, particularly Catholic Exclusivists, believe the problematic language of this passage cannot be so easily dismissed. One of the fiercest critics of this document, Bishop Athanasius Schneider, confronted the pope directly regarding this passage. During an *ad limina* visit to Rome after the Abu Dhabi Declaration was released, Schneider asked the pontiff to "retract that statement of the interreligious document of Abu Dhabi, which relativizes the uniqueness of faith in Jesus Christ."[211] Schneider relates that Pope Francis told him that "one must explain the phrase in the Abu Dhabi document regarding the diversity of religions in the sense of the 'permissive will of God.'"[212] Yet when Bishop Schneider asked, in verbal and later in written form, for the pope to make an official public state-

---

[211] Diane Montagna, "EXCLUSIVE: Bishop Schneider Says Vatican Is Betraying 'Jesus Christ as the Only Savior of Mankind,'" LifeSiteNews, August 26, 2019, https://www.lifesitenews.com/news/bishop-schneider-vatican-is-betraying-jesus-christ-as-the-only-savior-of-mankind.

[212] Montagna, "Bishop Schneider Says Vatican Is Betraying."

ment to this effect, no public response was given by the Vatican or the pope.

Perhaps the pope did intend to refer to the permissive will of God in the Abu Dhabi Declaration, but that is hard to reconcile with the plain sense of the text. The plurality of religions is just one item on a list of things "willed by God," including sex and the color of one's skin. If the list refers to God's permissive will, then being a man or a woman is not a result of the active will of God. That would fly in the face of fundamental Christian teaching, that "When God created man, he made him in the likeness of God. Male and female he created them, and he blessed them and named them Man when they were created" (Gen. 5:1-2). The same Scriptures that proclaim the differentiated sexes as part of God's active will also make clear that Religious Pluralism is the most evil result of the Fall. Putting sex differences and the plurality of religions on the same footing in terms of the will of God suggests either that the plurality of religions is actively willed by God or that sex differences are not God's active will. Neither belief is in keeping with historic Christian teaching.

Regardless of how theological specialists try to explain this statement, in practical terms the average person (who isn't well-versed in theological nuances) comes away with the plain meaning: God wants the plurality of religions. And if God wants many religions, it's hard to argue that one religion is superior or "more true" than another.

Far from making any public statement to discourage this interpretation, a year and a half after the Declaration, Pope Francis releases the encyclical *Fratelli Tutti* with many of the same themes:

> In this case, I have felt particularly encouraged by the Grand Imam Ahmad Al-Tayyeb, with whom I met in

Abu Dhabi, where we declared that "God has created all human beings equal in rights, duties and dignity, and has called them to live together as brothers and sisters." This was no mere diplomatic gesture, but a reflection born of dialogue and common commitment. The present Encyclical takes up and develops some of the great themes raised in the Document that we both signed.[213]

Pope Francis neither disavows the apparent Religious Pluralism in the Abu Dhabi Declaration nor reinterprets the document's plain meaning. No, this encyclical, if it doesn't outright embrace Religious Pluralism, sure sidles up to it flirtatiously.

The Church esteems the ways in which God works in other religions, and "rejects nothing of what is true and holy in these religions. She has a high regard for their manner of life and conduct, their precepts and doctrines which ... often reflect a ray of that truth which enlightens all men and women." Yet we Christians are very much aware that "if the music of the Gospel ceases to resonate in our very being, we will lose the joy born of compassion, the tender love born of trust, the capacity for reconciliation that has its source in our knowledge that we have been forgiven and sent forth. If the music of the Gospel ceases to sound in our homes, our public squares, our workplaces, our political and financial life, then we will no longer hear the strains that challenge us to defend the dignity of every man and woman." *Others drink from other sources.* For us the wellspring of human dignity and fraternity is in the Gospel of Jesus Christ. From it, there arises,

---

[213] Pope Francis, *Fratelli Tutti,* 5.

"for Christian thought and for the action of the Church, the primacy given to relationship, to the encounter with the sacred mystery of the other, to universal communion with the entire human family, as a vocation of all."[214]

Note that curious sentence: "Others drink from other sources." What does that mean? A plain reading of the text suggests that the pope is referring to the sources of other religions, sources different from the Gospel of Jesus Christ from which Christians "drink." So, other religions reject the Gospel, but use "other sources" and come to similar conclusions about human fraternity. This appears to be a green light for interpreting the Abu Dhabi Declaration as supporting Religious Pluralism.

Although the Abu Dhabi Declaration is a continuation of the Emphasis Shift, it's also a watershed in that it puts in print an endorsement (whether intentional or accidental) of Religious Pluralism. This unprecedented language is the culmination of decades of activities and statements which, practically if not officially, moved Catholics toward Religious Pluralism. It makes the implicit explicit. After treating other religions as equal to Catholicism for years, the Church now puts in writing the belief behind that course: that the plurality of religions is "willed by God."

And if God wills a multiplicity of religions, then following a specific religion becomes no more important than choosing a favorite dog breed. After all, the diversity of religions and the diversity of dog breeds are both "willed by God." You can debate with your friends which you prefer, but at the end of the day everyone knows it's a matter of personal preference. Catholic, Muslim, or even atheist—what does it matter?

---

[214] Pope Francis, *Fratelli Tutti*, 277, emphasis added.

V. The Impact

The Emphasis Shift that has led to the rise of religious indifference within the Church did not originate with any single statement by a pope or book by a Catholic theologian. No, it set in like a thick fog, formed from the words of Church documents, the treatises of influential theologians, and the actions of popes. This Emphasis Shift radically altered what it means to be Catholic, with three primary effects.

First, it has changed the beliefs of average Catholics. Even if Church leaders have been careful to (usually) not cross the line into heresy in their embrace of Inclusivism, most Catholics have not been so reticent. They've embraced Religious Pluralism with gusto, and the fruit is religious indifference.

Second, the Emphasis Shift and its resulting religious indifference have severely handicapped the missionary spirit of the Church. The Church that once blazed missionary trails across the world now seeks only to sit on the sidelines with everyone else. Although many Church leaders speak of a "New Evangelization," the reality is that most Catholics have no desire to convert people to the Church, precisely because religious indifference has neutered any desire to proclaim the Gospel.

DEADLY INDIFFERENCE

The Emphasis Shift and its aftermath also decimated day-to-day life in the Catholic parish, where most Catholics have their most direct (and sometimes only) contact with the Church. Parishes have mutated from waystations on the path to salvation to social clubs with a religious veneer. Due to religious indifference, most parishes today no longer seek the salvation of souls, contenting themselves with "community-building" and fighting for popular social causes.

19

Changing Our Beliefs

The massive Emphasis Shift of the past sixty years is comprised of three aspects: (1) from proclamation to dialogue; (2) from emphasizing the Church's uniqueness to presenting her as one option among many; and (3) from warning against errors to promoting the commonalities between Catholicism and other religions. Theologically, the Shift resulted in more hopeful attitudes about someone achieving salvation outside the visible boundaries of the Church. Practically, the Emphasis Shift engendered a number of unprecedented events in the history of the Church, including an interreligious prayer gathering held by the pope and a papal document that appears to endorse Religious Pluralism. These are the results at the highest levels of the Church. How about for the man in the pew?

One thing is clear: Religious Pluralism reigns. In 2008 the Pew Research Center polled Americans about whether religions other than their own can lead someone to Heaven.[215]

---

[215] Pew Research Center, "Many Americans Say Other Faiths Can Lead to Eternal Life," December 18, 2008, https://www.pewforum.org/2008/12/18/many-americans-say-other-faiths-can-lead-to-eternal-life/.

Here is the percentage of white Catholics who answered "No" (the historic Catholic answer) when asked if any of these religions can "lead to eternal life." (For some reason, the poll only subdivided white Catholics, and not all Catholics, from the overall numbers.)

Can the following religion lead to eternal life?	Percent of white Catholics answering "No"
Protestantism	6
Judaism	12
Islam	20
Hinduism	16

In other words, the vast majority of white Catholics believe that religions other than Catholicism can lead one to Heaven, which is a fundamental tenet of Religious Pluralism. Note that the question is not in the form of, "Can a member of [X religion] be saved?" but rather, "Can [X religion] lead to eternal life?" In other words, can the *practice* of another religion be the means by which someone is saved?

Compared with other Christian groups, Catholics are generally more confident about other religions leading to salvation. For example, when asked if Islam can lead to eternal life, only 20 percent of white Catholics in the poll answered "No." But other Christians, particularly Evangelical Protestant Christians, are much more skeptical:

Can Islam lead to eternal life?	Percent of each group answering "No"
White Evangelicals	45
White Mainline Protestants	26
Black Protestants	25

Further, when asked "Can *many religions* lead to eternal life?" 84 percent of white Catholics answered "Yes." Of those 84 percent, a vast majority (88 percent) responded that at least one non-Christian religion can lead to eternal life.

A few years later, the Pew Research Center conducted a similar poll.[216] When asked whether "many religions can lead to eternal life," 79 percent of all Catholics (not just white Catholics this time) answered "Yes." Among all Christian groups, this was the highest percentage answering "Yes." (Only 52 percent of Evangelical Protestants, for example, answered "Yes.")

So most Catholics in America (and there is little evidence to suggest that Catholics in other countries believe differently) do *not* believe that "outside the Church there is no salvation," in spite of the fact that EENS is still the official teaching of the Church. The Church's Emphasis Shift has led to a majority of Catholics' *change in belief.*

These poll numbers correspond to my own anecdotal evidence. For more than two decades I've been involved in Catholic evangelization at the individual, parish, and diocesan levels. I've led many evangelization projects and given hundreds of

[216] Pew Research Center, "U.S. Public Becoming Less Religious."

presentations on the subject. The biggest barrier to getting Catholics to evangelize is apathy: they simply don't see the need to share their faith with others. When pressed, most admit that they don't believe their non-Catholic loved ones are in any danger of going to Hell. The typical belief can be summed up like this: "As long as you are a good person, you will go to Heaven."

I remember once organizing a door-to-door evangelization campaign for a parish. Upon hearing about the event, one of the regular parishioners asked me, "Are we really that desperate for new members?" She could not see any other reason one would try to get others to become Catholic. Why bother, when other religions are just as good? Similarly, after my talks on the need for Catholics to evangelize, often audience members responded that we shouldn't try to convert non-Catholics to Catholicism. To do so would be offensive. That statement would usually be followed by a declaration that "we don't do that anymore," meaning, since Vatican II.

The Pluralist theological beliefs of most Catholics today are in direct contradiction to historic Catholic teaching. These erroneous beliefs have decimated the Church's missionary efforts as well as the life of the typical Catholic parish.

20

Failure of the New Evangelization

Less than two decades after the Emphasis Shift began, Church leaders realized something was wrong. By the early 1980s, the missionary drive that had propelled the Church to conquer much of the known world for Christ had all but disappeared. People were pouring out of the Church in record numbers, and fewer and fewer people were entering the Church. Missionary orders were vanishing. Something had to be done. Pope John Paul II had an idea: he called for a "New Evangelization."

Trying to Reverse the Decline

The first time the pope used this phrase was in a 1983 address to the Catholic bishops of Latin America. He said to them, "The commemoration of the half millennium of evangelization will gain its full energy if it is a commitment, not to re-evangelize but to a New Evangelization, new in its ardor, methods and expression."[217] Over the next decade, the phrase "New Evangelization" became

---

[217] Pope John Paul II, Address to CELAM (Opening Address of the Nineteenth General Assembly of CELAM, March 9, 1983, Port-au-Prince, Haiti), *L'Osservatore Romano* English edition 16/780, April 18, 1983, no. 9.

more common and eventually was adopted as a catchphrase representing the Church's renewed efforts to evangelize.

The New Evangelization also came to represent a contrast with the "old" evangelization; i.e., how things were done before the Emphasis Shift. Although it was the Emphasis Shift that dried up the Church's missionary spirit, the New Evangelization would nonetheless embrace the Emphasis Shift, not shun it. Instead of returning to old methods of evangelization, the New Evangelization would be a renewed effort to make the Emphasis Shift work. It became the Church's new mission.

Although the term is ambiguous, in practice, the New Evangelization has certain characteristics:

- *It is nonconfrontational.* The New Evangelization focuses on highlighting the positive in the world and in the Church and shies away from critiquing others and their beliefs.
- *Dialogue with the culture.* The New Evangelization is about finding ways to embrace the culture as much as possible in an effort to reach people "where they're at."
- A *focus on fallen-away, nonpracticing Catholics.* Due to the massive increase in the number of baptized Catholics who no longer practice their faith, the New Evangelization is particularly geared toward bringing these individuals back to the practice of the Faith.
- A *de-emphasis of eternal consequences.* The New Evangelization rarely talks of the dangers of Hell or even the joys of Heaven. Instead its focus is on building relationships here on earth: with Jesus, the Church, and those around us.[218]

---

[218] For example, in the USCCB document, *Disciples Called to Witness: The New Evangelization* (2012), the word "Hell" is never used, and the word "Heaven" is used only once, in reference to

- A *soft touch with non-Catholics*. Instead of urging non-Catholics to become Catholic, the New Evangelization highlights the extraordinary means of salvation.

We can see in these characteristics that the New Evangelization is a product, not a repudiation, of the Emphasis Shift.

By the turn of the twenty-first century, the New Evangelization became ensconced as *the* methodology for evangelization and missionary work. It was touted by Church leaders, both clerical and lay, as the way the Church would reverse her declining numbers, both by inspiring Catholics to stay in the Church and by attracting fallen-away Catholics to come back. The New Evangelization would make the twenty-first century the Catholic century.

Sadly, twenty years into this century we see that this has not happened. In fact, since 2000 an even more precipitous decline has occurred. For example, we can look to infant Baptisms. Baptisms are a key indicator of the health of the Church, as even marginally practicing Catholics will usually baptize their children. A falling number of Baptisms indicates that fewer young Catholics are practicing their faith on any level.

Let's look at the tragic numbers of U.S. infant Baptisms in the chart on the following page.[219]

After 1970 we witness a steep decline until 1975, followed by a small 11 percent increase over the next twenty-five years

---

Jesus ascending to Heaven. The word "relationship," in context of "with Jesus, with the Church, and with others," is mentioned more than a dozen times.

[219] Data in charts taken from "Frequently Requested Church Statistics," Center for Applied Research in the Apostolate, https://cara.georgetown.edu/frequently-requested-church-statistics/.

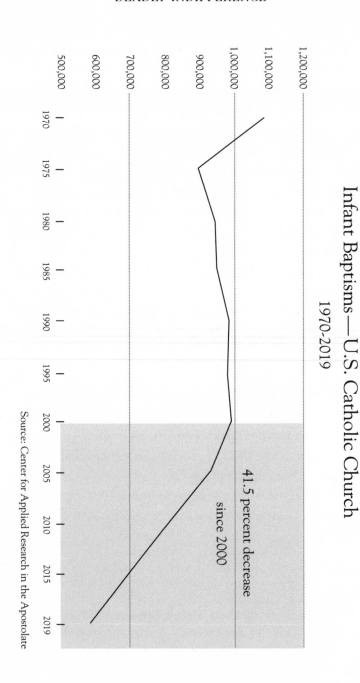

Infant Baptisms—U.S. Catholic Church
1970-2019

41.5 percent decrease
since 2000

Source: Center for Applied Research in the Apostolate

(even this small increase from 1975 to 2000 isn't good news, as the Catholic population grew by 31 percent during this same time period). However, starting in 2000 — when the New Evangelization was really taking off — the numbers dropped like a stone. Further, the decline in infant Baptisms is actually worse than the chart shows, for it doesn't take into account that during this time the overall population of Americans was rapidly increasing. Overall, since 1970, the U.S. population has grown by 60 percent, but the number of annual infant Baptisms has decreased by 46 percent.

Obviously, there are many factors for this drop after 2000 (the sexual abuse crisis being a primary culprit), but it's obvious that the New Evangelization has not accomplished what it was promoted to do. It has not kept Catholics in the Church or inspired fallen-away Catholics to return. The New Evangelization's embrace of the Emphasis Shift has made it fundamentally unable to overcome the widespread religious indifference that underlies the declining numbers.

How the New Evangelization Fails to Evangelize

When Catholics no longer believe there are fundamental differences between Catholicism and other religions, they will be less likely to think it's important to practice the Faith. Further, they will be less likely to invite non-Catholics to do so. By looking more closely at each of the New Evangelization's characteristics, we find that religious indifference underlies each one, handicapping the effectiveness of the entire New Evangelization project.

First, the New Evangelization is *nonconfrontational.* This sounds positive. After all, no one likes someone attacking his faith or condemning him to Hell. But what if some confrontation is needed for effective evangelization? St. John the Baptist made the call to repentance a foundation of his preaching (cf. Mark 1:4). In the first papal sermon, St. Peter accused the listening crowd of killing the promised Messiah and urged them to repent (cf. Acts 2:14-36). Catholic missionaries throughout the centuries have confronted pagans with the dangers of Hell for the unconverted. These missionaries understood that it would be better for their hearers to face some uncomfortableness now than eternal damnation later.

The taint of indifference kills any willingness for confrontation in the New Evangelization. If other religions lead to Heaven as well, then the stakes have been greatly reduced. Religion becomes a matter for personal preference, not eternal salvation. Thus, Catholic evangelization takes on the feel of a good-natured discussion about whether someone prefers Coke or Pepsi. Without eternal consequences on the line, there is no reason to be confrontational. Instead, we can focus solely on the positives in other religions and emphasize our commonalities with them.

Second, the New Evangelization embraces the key methodology of the Emphasis Shift: *dialogue*. This dialogue goes beyond religious topics and beliefs to secular culture. Instead of condemning problems in the culture, the New Evangelization looks to engage the culture via dialogue. This usually means *embracing* as much of the surrounding culture as possible. Instead of setting the Church apart from the world, the New Evangelization seeks to be part of it.

This effort at dialoguing with the culture means, in practice, becoming as much like the culture as possible and praising it whenever possible. Yet, if there is so much good in the culture, and the culture can be found both inside and outside the Church, then why bother to become Catholic? If Catholicism is made more culturally relevant, then there's no need to bother with attending Sunday Mass, since you can embrace the culture more fully by skipping Mass and indulging in cultural entertainments. Indifferent to the religious dangers inherent in secular culture, the New Evangelization undercuts a Catholic's defense against it and does little to draw non-Catholics to the Church.

The third aspect of the New Evangelization, and what in many ways makes it "new," is the *focus on fallen-away or barely practicing Catholics* instead of non-Catholics. This is new because the situation is unprecedented: never before have such a massive number of people in the world identified as former Catholics! So it's understandable that Church leaders feel a need to focus on this large demographic. Yet this focus has also become a "safe" form of evangelization; the low-hanging fruit that excuses Catholics from trying to convert non-Catholics.

Think about the difference between trying to convert a Muslim co-worker, for example, and trying to convert your neighbor who grew up Catholic. Reaching out to the Muslim is fraught with difficulties: he may be offended, you might lose your job, and you will likely be branded as pushy. It goes against all the instincts fostered during the Emphasis Shift. Inviting a fallen-away Catholic to come back to the Church, however, has none of those pitfalls. A fallen-away Catholic is an acceptable target for evangelization, because he is already one of "ours," whereas focusing on someone who did not grow up Catholic seems to be engaging in the dreaded "proselytism."

I witnessed this reticence first-hand when I planned door-to-door campaigns for our parish. I've already described the woman who accosted our pastor, saying, "Are we that desperate for members?" But I also encountered resistance from many well-meaning Catholics who felt the Church should only give attention to bringing former Catholics back into the fold. Sadly, an implicit indifference is the foundation of this attitude, for it reduces religion to cultural upbringing. It's acceptable to reach out to people who were raised Catholic to become practicing Catholics, but it's offensive to try to convert non-Catholics to the Church.

Fourth, no aspect of the New Evangelization is more impacted by religious indifference than its *de-emphasis on eternal consequences*. We've already seen how this de-emphasis undergirds the nonconfrontational attitude of the New Evangelization. But it also shapes the message that is spread. In most cases, the New Evangelization presents Catholicism as the best way to live here on earth. The Catholic Faith brings joy and fulfillment to one's life by having a relationship with Jesus and His Church, although what this relationship entails or why to even have it in the first place is often less clear. Sharing the Gospel of Eternal Life becomes an exercise in motivational speaking. Any eternal consequences—whether one will spend eternity in Heaven or Hell—are kept quietly in the closet.

De-emphasizing eternal consequences is the direct result of the Emphasis Shift's focus on the positive elements of religion and its excessive hopefulness regarding the possibility of salvation for the non-Catholic. If it's likely that most people are going to Heaven, whether they are Catholic or not, then evangelization efforts need only focus on this world, not the next. If we cannot (or will not) mention the eternal consequences of what religion one belongs to, then we are left simply to communicate how Catholicism can make one's life better. Evangelization devolves into self-help advertising.

Finally, the New Evangelization has a *soft touch* when it comes to inviting non-Catholics to consider converting to Catholicism, often even shying away from inviting non-Catholics at all. In the USCCB document *Go and Make Disciples: A National Plan and*

Strategy for Catholic Evangelization in the United States, the first statement under "In Sharing the Gospel with Others" we read,

> The Holy Spirit also evangelizes through our attempts to reach those who have given up the practice of their Catholic faith for one reason or another and those who have no family of faith. Many in our Catholic community know family members, friends, and neighbors who do not have or practice faith.[220]

Even when, a few paragraphs later, the document states, "People of other non-Christian religions also have the right to hear the Gospel, as missionaries have brought it over the centuries," it is followed by the statement, "Interreligious dialogue presents an opportunity to learn about other religious traditions and to explain our own. Such dialogue, however, must never be a camouflage for proselytizing."[221] In other words, Catholics must walk on eggshells, never giving even the slightest suggestion that one religion might be superior to another. This soft touch is a direct result of the Emphasis Shift making ordinary the extraordinary means of salvation. Instead of focusing on the norm—that one must be a visible member of the Church to be saved (*extra Ecclesiam nulla salus*)—the New Evangelization strives to assure non-Catholics that they most likely will be saved without visible membership. A non-Catholic who is talking to a New Evangelization Catholic will typically walk away without feeling at all uncomfortable about his chances of salvation by means of his current religion.

---

[220] United States Conference of Catholic Bishops (USCCB), *Go and Make Disciples: A National Plan and Strategy for Catholic Evangelization in the United States*, November 18, 1992, 38.

[221] USCCB, *Go and Make Disciples*, 44.

The New Evangelization in Practice

We can see the New Evangelization in practice by examining another YouTube interview with Bishop Robert Barron. This time it is an interview between Barron and a practicing Protestant Christian. We will look at Barron's responses because he is considered by most to be the *de facto* American leader of the New Evangelization. At the time of the interview, he was the Chairman of the United States Conference of Catholic Bishops Committee on Evangelization and Catechesis—literally the bishops' point-man on evangelization. No cleric has done more in recent years to promote the New Evangelization, and most advocates of the New Evangelization look to him as a role model, perhaps even *the* role model when it comes to evangelization.

In September 2020, Bishop Barron appeared on *Capturing Christianity*, a popular Protestant YouTube channel, for an interview with founder Cameron Bertuzzi on a range of topics.[222] At one point, Bertuzzi asks Barron point-blank: "Should I become Catholic?"

After a brief pause, Barron answers, "Yes, is my blunt answer." But then he immediately follows with, "Now if you want to press that … ," but then Bertuzzi interrupts him by asking, "Why?" But from later context in the interview, it's clear that Barron was about to start talking about the extraordinary means of salvation available to non-Catholics. Barron's "yes" is an immediately qualified "yes."

When Bertuzzi asks "Why?" (should he become Catholic), Barron answers, "Because it's the fullness of truth and I want

---

[222] "A Protestant Asks Bishop Barron if He Should Become Catholic," *Capturing Christianity* YouTube Channel, September 25, 2020, https://youtu.be/HEkOV9LsCTo.

to share that with you. It's something I've come to love and reverence as the fullness of truth ... all the gifts Christ wants his people to have.... Why wouldn't I want to share those with you? Why wouldn't I want to offer all that to you?" No mention of Heaven—let alone Hell. Barron doesn't even give a direct answer to the question, "Why should I be Catholic?" Instead he seems to answer the question, "Why do *you* want me to become Catholic?" or "Why are *you* Catholic?" Barron's sole focus is on his positive experience of Catholicism and defending why he would want someone else to experience that.

Then, before Bertuzzi has a chance to say anything else, Barron returns to saying, "Now, if you want to press the issue ..." Before looking at what the "issue" in question is, note that Bertuzzi is *not* pressing any issue; it's Barron who's making sure to bring one up. So what is Barron so anxious to say?

> Does that mean I'm [i.e., Bertuzzi] damned? No, no, that's not Catholic teaching. You know that a non-Catholic, even a non-Christian, *can* be saved.... I'm not saying *will* be saved.... They *can* be saved; that's the Catholic teaching.

Barron then spends a few more minutes expounding on all the ways a non-Catholic can be saved, particularly mentioning *Lumen Gentium* 16, which we have seen is a foundational text for the Church's Emphasis Shift regarding the means of salvation.

Note the direction of Barron's answer. When asked point blank, "Should I become Catholic?" Barron initially, yet briefly, answers "Yes," but then focuses his answer on all the reasons Bertuzzi would probably be saved anyway if he doesn't become Catholic. As an Expansive Inclusivist, Barron is strident in making sure Bertuzzi knows he *can* be saved without becoming

Catholic. What is any listener's take-away from all this? That being Catholic is a personal preference, and little more.

I'm not giving this example of Bishop Barron in order to critique him personally. Nor am I questioning his good intentions. I am aware that Barron has influenced some Catholics to practice their faith more fully and perhaps some non-Catholics to become Catholic. It's as the representative of the New Evangelization in the United States that I include him here.

Barron didn't necessarily say anything theologically wrong, although his answers could easily lead average Catholics to adopt theologically heretical views, namely, Pluralism. Yet it's important to see how in following the New Evangelization methodology (and adopting its underlying Emphasis Shift), Barron gives his interviewer and listeners a generally hopeful view regarding the salvation of non-Catholics. His answer shows how the New Evangelization works in practice and how the Emphasis Shift has influenced that methodology. Most Catholics now believe that, Catholic or non-Catholic, most people will likely get to Heaven. Because of this, the New Evangelization has failed to reverse in any substantial way the disturbing downward demographic trends in the Church.

21

The Sad State of Today's Catholic Parish

It's 1949 and Edward Sullivan is forty years old. He describes himself as an active member of his Catholic parish. He helps organize the Holy Name Society's annual Men's Eucharistic Procession that draws thousands of participants each year. When his early-morning milk route schedule allows, he is a regular at the first morning Mass. His oldest son has advanced as an altar server to the level of Master of Ceremonies, while his youngest has just served his first Mass as an acolyte. All five of his children attend the parish school, where they are taught largely by religious sisters, some of whom he knew as his own teachers. His wife volunteers in the kindergarten at the school, sings in the parish choir, and supplements the family income as a Latin tutor for high schoolers. Since life revolves around their faith, it naturally revolves around their parish.

Now it's 2019 and Jason Sullivan is forty years old. He, too, describes himself as an active member of his parish. He helps organize the annual parish festival, where this year's beer sales alone will raise enough funds to repave the parish parking lot. An EMT, he volunteers monthly when the parish offers blood pressure screenings. Each Tuesday his daughter and son attend religious education classes, except when they have soccer games that night. His daughter is an altar server, but his son lost interest after a few years of serving. Jason's wife is a nurse in a rehabilitation center and often works weekends, so the family isn't always able to make it to Mass together on Sunday. Mass is just one of the many activities on a crowded family calendar.

The dramatic differences in parish life between these two scenes are undeniable. In the first, parish life revolves around spiritual activities and devotions; in the second, the focus is on, well, just activity and busyness. I argue that these differences trace back to the Emphasis Shift that led to the rise of Religious Pluralism and religious indifference, and that has in turn called into question the fundamental purpose of a parish.

The Purpose of a Parish

What *is* the purpose of a parish? The Church's canon law defines a parish this way:

> A parish is a certain community of Christ's faithful stably established within a particular Church, whose pastoral care, under the authority of the diocesan Bishop, is entrusted to a parish priest as its proper pastor. (Can. 515.1)

> A lawfully established parish has juridical personality by virtue of the law itself. (Can. 515.3)

So, a parish is a community of Christ's faithful, typically set up to cover a specific territory (cf. Can. 518), and it is a "juridical personality," which is legal language saying the parish is an entity created by the law and unto which certain laws apply. That's helpful for knowing *what* a parish is, but it doesn't answer the question of *why* a parish exists. What is its purpose?

In chapter 1 I noted that the last canon in the Code of Canon Law states that in the Church the "salvation of souls ... must always be the supreme law" (Can. 1752). In other words, *all* laws in the Church are directed toward the one purpose of our salvation. Applying this fitting principle to the juridical entity of a parish, the ultimate purpose of a parish becomes clear: *the salvation of souls*. It exists for no other reason.

Parishes are just convenient structures the Church uses to organize herself, and she does so for the purpose of saving souls. The pope or even each bishop can't interact with all the faithful. Therefore the Church sets up parishes, and appoints priests as pastors, in an attempt to reach out to every soul to lead each one to salvation. Something that is little known by Catholics today is that a pastor of a parish is responsible for every soul who lives within his geographic parish boundaries — not just the parishioners, or even just the Catholics, but *every* soul. This is because parishes were created as an organizational method to save everyone, no matter their current religious state.

Yet today, if you ask the average Catholic what the purpose of the parish is, the salvation of souls is likely not high on the list, if it is there at all. Some answers might be related to that purpose: "To celebrate Mass," or "To help us be better Catholics." But other answers will not be related, and many will likely point instead to community-building: "To offer activities for families" or "To help Catholics connect," for example. Some Catholics might respond with answers focused on this world: "To work for social justice" or "To lift up the poor." Very few Catholics will answer that the parish's single purpose is to help us gain Heaven.

How Indifference Has Seeped In

This misunderstanding of the purpose of a parish is a direct result of religious indifference among Catholics. An excessive focus on the extraordinary means of salvation, leading to a widespread acceptance of Religious Pluralism, has led to most Catholics forgetting "salvation" is a primary purpose of Catholicism in general and therefore the Catholic parish. If we assume most people are going to Heaven, whether Catholic or not, then what help toward salvation do we need from our parish?

We can see this indifference seeping into every aspect of parish life.

First, most parishes do all they can to avoid controversial topics, even if those topics can directly impact someone's salvation. Avoiding controversy is standard policy for most non-political groups, such as the Elks Club or the local Little League. Controversy can turn people away, and so groups shy away from anything that might cause offense. Parishes have adopted this policy too, thanks to religious indifference. When was the last time you heard Hell, contraception, or divorce mentioned at your parish? If preaching on Hell might turn people away, why bring it up? Almost no one is going there anyway.

The increase in parish-sponsored non-religious activities can also be traced to religious indifference. Many parishes offer a plethora of activities that serve no direct religious purpose: youth sports, health events, and spaghetti dinners. None of these activities are bad in and of themselves, but this "building community" often shifts from *serving* the primary purpose of a parish (the salvation of souls) to *being* the primary purpose of a parish. Parishes seem more like social clubs than waystations to salvation.

This change often happens without anyone noticing. Most parish staff would deny the purpose of their parish is just sports and festivals. Yet when one scrutinizes how much time and resources are allocated to these activities vs. activities directly related to the salvation of souls, it's hard not to wonder what the real purpose of the parish is. And again, it is indifference that encourages this evolution, as it downplays the vital and unique role of a Catholic spiritual life in each person's life. It makes primary what is secondary, and secondary what is primary.

Religious indifference has also influenced parishes' interaction with their surrounding communities. I mentioned previously the comments of Derek Worlock, Archbishop of Liverpool, who said:

> I was brought up not to enter a Protestant building, let alone take an active part in what took place there. Even to be present at the funeral or wedding of a non-Catholic relation required ecclesiastical permission and due care not to give the impression of taking part in the recitation of Protestant prayers or in hymn singing.[223]

Today, however, Catholic parishes usually have close relations with the churches, synagogues, and mosques in their neighborhoods and regularly engage in shared activities. For example, at a parish I used to attend there was an annual Christmas musical that was co-sponsored by our parish, a Presbyterian church, and a Mormon ward. The event rotated between the three sites each year and each congregation encouraged its members to attend. Quite a difference from the youthful days of Archbishop Worlock! If you take your children to this event every Christmas, aren't you a little like the Yankee fan taking his son to a Red Sox game each year? What's the message?

The focus on ecumenism and interreligious dialogue, based in religious indifference, also cripples the evangelistic outreach of a parish. I've mentioned already my efforts to hold door-to-door evangelization campaigns in my old parish. Although there were a core group of parishioners who supported it, many others felt it

---

[223] Quoted in Bullivant, *Mass Exodus*, 98-99.

was unnecessary, even unseemly. To ask non-Catholics to convert is seen as gauche, something to which only Mormons or Jehovah's Witnesses would stoop. Typical Catholic parishes have absolutely no outreach that urges people to convert, for they don't even see that as something Catholics should do. They hold RCIA programs for potential adult converts, but these take place after-the-fact; they are not intended to reach out and produce more converts.

Religious indifference has also transformed the overall "vibe" of parishes. This is hard for Catholics who have only attended parishes impacted by the Emphasis Shift to perceive. The usual feel we encounter in today's Catholic parish seems normal now. Yet looking at parish life before the Emphasis Shift can give us a hint that things used to be different, both in the activities and in the very bones of the church. Anyone entering a Catholic church a century ago would know immediately, "This is a Catholic church." It would be obvious from the architecture to the statues to the stained-glass windows to the smell of incense dominating the church to the music during Mass to the devotions being prayed.

Now when one enters many suburban parishes it's not clear, aside from, perhaps, a hanging crucifix and a picture of the pope, if it's a Catholic church or a Protestant church or even a local community hall. The activities might be as generic as a book club or a blood drive. If there's one word to describe many Catholic churches today, it's "beige." Nothing says, "We're Catholic and proud of it!" Instead, it blandly whimpers, "We're a local community organization." That's religious indifference in a nutshell; there's little that's truly unique about Catholicism that is promoted or displayed. If our friend Edward Sullivan from 1949 were to enter a modern Catholic parish, he in his confusion would likely end up asking for directions to the local Catholic church.

Religious indifference has gravely harmed the Church at every level, but nowhere is its awful impact more significant than in the typical Catholic parish. It has transformed the House of God into a community center. It has been an insidious plague on the life of the Catholic parish, sucking all the religious energy out of it. Instead of places devoted to the salvation of souls, parishes have become social clubs, with little knowledge of their very purpose.

VI. The Way Forward

In this book we have detailed how the Church lost sight of her mission: by a massive Emphasis Shift that led to an embrace of religious indifference among Catholics. But how do we recover her mission? How can the Catholic Church overcome this indifference, return to presenting herself as the way to salvation, and fulfill Christ's command to "make disciples of all nations, baptizing them in the name of the Father and of the Son and of the Holy Spirit" (Matt. 28:19)?

First, Catholics, particularly Church leaders, must recognize the need to change the status quo. In dioceses and parishes around the world, most things are done "because that's how they've always been done," which usually means that's how they've been done since the 1970s. Inertia is the most powerful force guiding chanceries and parish offices (as well as the Vatican). Few people even consider questioning the prevailing Religious Pluralism or the ecumenical and interreligious activities that promote it. The extraordinary means of salvation continue to be made for all intents and purposes ordinary means. We've seen, however, that "how things are done" has led to disastrous results.

Overcoming the status quo often entails toppling sacred cows and stepping on toes. It involves re-teaching people how to understand the organization's mission and how it operates. We will have to convince people to rethink what it means to be Catholic. It's a difficult task. But if we desire to renew the Church and recover her mission, we have to embrace this challenge for the sake of souls.

To overcome religious indifference among Catholics, we face three main tasks. First, we must teach Catholics the Church's role in the process of salvation, and the historical understanding of the possibility of salvation for non-Catholics. Second, Catholics must learn how to evangelize effectively, which means re-embracing old, proven techniques over those muddied by religious indifference. Finally, Catholic parishes must remake themselves as waystations on the path to salvation, leaving behind the Elks Club feel. We'll look at each of these tasks in turn in the following chapters.

22

Understanding Church Teaching on Salvation

Before the Church can take practical steps to recover her mission, Catholics must undertake a theological and attitudinal readjustment. Otherwise, any practical steps will be built on a shaky foundation. In chapter 9 I introduced the Salvation Spectrum to represent the range of differences we find among Catholic views on the salvation of non-Catholics. Let's study it again (see next page).

One vital aspect of this spectrum is that it represents both theology and attitude. Too often when Catholics disagree they spend endless hours debating whether a position is in conformity with magisterial teaching. That's an important question, for sure, but it's not the only important one. As we've seen, too often a Church leader or theologian who accepts Catholic magisterial teaching speaks and acts in ways that foster religious indifference. In fact, the dominant school in the Church today—Inclusivism, which accepts magisterial Church teaching on the necessity of Christ and His Church for salvation—often manifests practical Pluralism, which rejects magisterial Church teaching. Even in its more benign forms, Inclusivism fosters indifference (and Pluralism) among average Catholics.

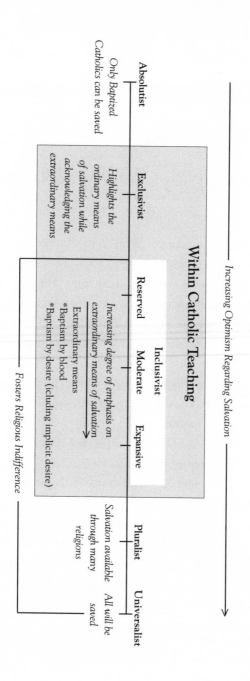

Salvation Spectrum

Increasing Optimism Regarding Salvation

Absolutist
Only Baptized Catholics can be saved

Exclusivist
Highlights the ordinary means of salvation while acknowledging the extraordinary means

Within Catholic Teaching

Inclusivist

Reserved

Moderate

Expansive

Increasing degree of emphasis on extraordinary means of salvation

Extraordinary means
*Baptism by blood
*Baptism by desire (icluding implicit desire)

Pluralist
Salvation available through many religions

Universalist
All will be saved

Fosters Religious Indifference

A Return to Exclusivism

The only school that balances the theological need to affirm Church teaching while maintaining the practical attitude that doesn't foster indifference is *Exclusivism*. Exclusivism acknowledges that God can work through the extraordinary means of salvation — Baptism of blood and Baptism of desire — but focuses on our duty and obligation to seek the ordinary means — water Baptism and visible membership in the Catholic Church. Exclusivism avoids the danger of Absolutism (believing that only water-baptized Catholics can be saved), as well as the dangers of Pluralism and Universalism. It also re-energizes the Church's missionary zeal which propelled her for 1,900 years. *Catholics need to embrace Exclusivism again if we are to regain the Church's mission.*

What does this entail practically? The first and most important task is promoting a proper attitude toward the extraordinary means of salvation. We should neither *emphasize* nor *presume* them, but treat them as they are: extra-ordinary (i.e., outside the ordinary) ways in which God can save someone. Emphasizing these extraordinary means makes them ordinary; it shifts our focus away from our own obligations to be baptized and be visible members of the Catholic Church. We are obligated to invite, even urge, non-Catholics to become Catholic; to seek out the ordinary way which God has given for salvation.

Imagine the following scenario. You and your friend live in New York City and you both need to get to Los Angeles. He can't afford a plane ticket and doesn't own a car, so he decides to walk there. He's also out-of-shape and on crutches due to a broken foot. You, however, have a new car that's gassed up and ready to go. You could say nothing and let your friend try to walk to California. You could even encourage him to do so. After all, it's *possible* that he could make it. However, this would be quite extraordinary, and you have a sure, ordinary, way for him to get there: he can ride in your car with you. So should you spend your time emphasizing that it's possible for your friend to walk to Los Angeles, or should you urge him to ride in the car with you?

The reasonableness of Exclusivism can be seen by looking at it as a form of Pascal's Wager. In the original wager, Pascal argued that it was logical to live as if God exists, for if He does exist, you will be rewarded after death. And if God does not exist, there will be no negative consequences for living as if He does, since there will be no afterlife to worry about.

In a similar fashion, the Exclusivist argues it is logical to assume everyone must take the ordinary means of salvation, which is water Baptism and living as a practicing member of the Catholic Church. If you do take this route, God has promised that you will be saved. There are no negative consequences to using the ordinary means even if you could have been saved by extraordinary means because the ordinary means are *guaranteed* to bring you to salvation. But if you assume extraordinary means and they are not available in your particular situation, then you risk eternal damnation. It's clear that the ordinary means should be what are emphasized in all situations.

Exclusivism is also consistent with the historic attitude of Catholics. Pope Pius IX condemned the following errors that fostered religious indifference as they crept into nineteenth-century Catholic circles:

- Every man is free to embrace and profess that religion which, guided by the light of reason, he shall consider true.
- Man may, in the observance of any religion whatever, find the way of eternal salvation, and arrive at eternal salvation.

• Good hope at least is to be entertained of the eternal salvation of all those who are not at all in the true Church of Christ.

• Protestantism is nothing more than another form of the same true Christian religion, in which form it is given to please God equally as in the Catholic Church.[224]

Note in particular the third error listed: "Good hope at least is to be entertained of the eternal salvation of all those who are not at all in the true Church of Christ." The pope is preemptively condemning the belief of Hans Urs von Balthasar, a hope that all men might be saved (see chapter 10). Further, Pius IX contradicts the overall ethos of the entire school of Inclusivism, which insists on an overly hopeful attitude when it comes to the salvation of non-Catholics. The view of the Exclusivist Catholic is simply the dominant Catholic view throughout history.

Asking the Right Questions

Why the skepticism regarding the salvation of non-Catholics? After all, isn't God merciful? Why would he send someone to Hell simply because the person wasn't a visible member of the Church?

We need to realize that these very questions, so commonly asked today, imply the Inclusivist (if not Pluralist) mindset. They fix on what *God* can do rather than what *we* have been commanded to do. Picture a teenager whose dad is a judge. His dad tells him always to follow the law. But the son breaks the law, figuring his dad won't sentence him to any jail time, since he has the power to let him off. And yes, it's possible the dad will pardon his son, yet the son should have obeyed his father's command: don't break the law.

---

[224] Pope Pius IX, *Syllabus of Errors*, 15-18.

*So the important question is not, "Can God save non-Catholics?"
The important question is, "What has God asked us to do to be saved?"*
He has commanded us to be baptized by water and to be members
of His Church in order to be saved. Therefore, we need to obey
His command and leave the extraordinary means to His divine
mercy and judgment. Let's shift our emphasis back to the ordinary
means and stop treating the extraordinary means as ordinary.

The original Vatican II preparatory *schemata* give one example
of integrating an Exclusivist outlook with the realities of the modern world. These documents acknowledged the extraordinary
means, but they did not rest on them. In the *schema* on the Church,
one chapter is devoted to the necessity of the Church for salvation.
It first presses home the truth of *extra Ecclesiam nulla salus*, while
acknowledging that some people might be united to the Church
by an explicit desire. It particularly explores the connection of the
"separated brethren" (note it doesn't use the antiquated language
of "schismatics" and "heretics") but then urges conversion:

> The Church never ceases to pray that the separated
> brethren, showing themselves freely and spontaneously
> docile to the internal impulses of divine grace, may strive
> to leave that state in which they lack so many and such
> great heavenly gifts and aids for obtaining eternal salva-
> tion, gifts and aids which they alone may enjoy who are
> really members of the Church.[225]

In a chapter on ecumenism later in the document we find
repeated calls to bring people into the Catholic fold, something
that was completely missing from the final Vatican II document
on ecumenism:

---

[225] Preparatory Theological Commission, *De Ecclesia*, chap. 2.

Therefore, this Holy Synod approves the initiatives of Catholics by which separated brethren are being enlightened about the teaching and life of the Church so that even individually they may be drawn towards her, and it urges that such efforts be still further promoted.

This holy Synod admonishes all the faithful more and more by word and example to show the separated brethren that the fullness of revelation is truly and purely maintained only in the Catholic Church, and to do this in such a way that when finally our brothers are again linked with us, they may with us also possess the fullness of Christ's heritage.

This holy Synod warns all the faithful that there is need for great prudence in [ecumenical] activity lest, moved by a certain apostolic zeal but without knowledge, they be exposed to the danger of indifferentism or a so-called interconfessionalism or by an excited way of proceeding injure rather than serve the intended purpose.

This noble work of restoring the unity of all Christians in the one true faith and the one Church must become an ever greater part in the care of souls. Let all the faithful, together with the separated brethren, insistently pray God for this unity, and let them be convinced that the most effective means of opening a way for separated Christians to acknowledge and embrace the one Church of Christ is the faith of Catholics when it is confirmed by their honorable lives.[226]

---

[226] Preparatory Theological Commission, *De Ecclesia*, chap. 11.

Notice the focus on a Catholic's obligations: to strive to bring people into the Church and to work that everyone might be saved via the ordinary means which Christ has given us, i.e., visible membership in the Catholic Church. Sadly, like all the preparatory *schemata*, this document was discarded at the beginning of the first official session of Vatican II because of the push for the Emphasis Shift.

A Hard Road

Re-embracing Exclusivism will be difficult. We live in a pluralistic world and it's assumed we must be tolerant of the beliefs and practices of others. And Catholics *should* be tolerant, but tolerance does not equate to acceptance of false beliefs, nor does it preclude calls to conversion. As Bishop Athanasius Schneider wrote,

> Religious tolerance was always part of Catholic doctrine, even before the Council [Vatican II]. But Catholics cannot be in favor of other religions propagating their errors, because all religions that are not Catholic are erroneous, and God does not approve them, and so they are contrary to the will of God.... Therefore, Catholics must tolerate other religions but not promote them. This is an essential difference.[227]

Exclusivism is not incompatible with a religiously tolerant society. The Church can be Exclusivist again and still exist in harmony with a pluralistic world. But it's essential that she act not in ways that lead Catholics to religious indifference.

---

[227] Schneider, *Christus Vincit*, 85.

Re-embracing Exclusivism will also at times be uncomfortable. Catholics for decades have been trained, consciously and unconsciously, to never talk about their faith to others — especially to never challenge the beliefs of non-Catholics. Does re-embracing Exclusivism mean that we must condemn our non-Catholic friends as schismatics, heretics, and pagans? That we should shun them? Not at all. As we saw in the preparatory Vatican II *schemata*, there can be a balance between an Exclusivist outlook and an understanding of our current situation. The Exclusivist is driven to present to others the beauty and truth of Catholicism, and so he will find opportunities to do so. But how he responds to those opportunities will be shaped by our current culture. He will not treat all religions as equal, but he will understand that most people today do and therefore adapt his discussions about religion accordingly. Instead of being indifferent to the religion of others, however, he will be motivated to proclaim Catholicism. We'll get into the details of how that can be practically accomplished in the next chapter.

23

Bring Back the Old Evangelization

In order to reclaim the Church's mission, Catholics need to make a theological and attitudinal adjustment along the Salvation Spectrum, embracing the Exclusivist school. This is the foundation for moving forward, since our theology and our attitude drive our actions. However, reclaiming the Church's mission isn't just about having the correct theology or even the correct attitude; it requires putting that mission into practice. In these final two chapters we will look at some practical ways Catholics — both lay and clerical — can contribute to reclaiming the Church's mission. These suggestions are not intended to be comprehensive, as each person is in a unique situation. Instead they are to be a guide for determining how best to move forward and help reverse the Church's decline and bring about renewal.

As we've seen, the Church's Emphasis Shift led to religious indifference that decimated the practice of the Church's mission, and so we must reverse that Shift to recover it. We've seen that the Emphasis Shift was comprised of three primary aspects (see chapters 6-8); we must reverse all three aspects.

Return to Proclaiming

First the Church changed the way she related to the world. Rather than proclaiming the Gospel to the world, she sought dialogue with it. As much as official Church documents insisted that dialogue and proclamation should complement one another, in reality dialogue dominates the Church's outreach; there is no proclamation. The result of the shift from proclamation to dialogue has been devastating. How do Catholics return to proclaiming the Gospel to the world? Does it mean we all need to stand on the street corner haranguing passersby to convert? Not at all.

First we need to understand what it means to "proclaim the Gospel." More often than not, this means explaining to others how the Gospel has impacted one's own life, followed by an invitation for the other to embrace the Gospel as well. Proclamation is an ongoing conversation involving personal testimony, explanation of Catholic doctrine (including its more controversial aspects), critique of the errors of other religions, and an explicit call to conversion. This differs from modern-day "dialogue" in that it has as its driving force the conversion of non-Catholics to the Church. It is also unabashedly and unapologetically Catholic. It does not try to hide matters on which the Church differs from other religions; in fact, it often emphasizes those differences in order to make the distinctions clear.

The majority of official ecumenical and especially interreligious dialogues occurring today serve no purpose. In our modern world, it's easy to discover what other religions believe and how their adherents practice their religions. These official dialogues are now simply opportunities for religious leaders to socialize and affirm one another as members of equally valid religions. Officials spending countless hours trying to find every similarity between

Catholicism and Hinduism, for example, is a waste of time that only encourages religious indifference in the pews.

It might seem that I'm being too hard on these official "dialogues." However, I would argue that most dialogues face an insurmountable problem: no true end goal. High-cost symposiums and official meetings proliferate, but no true progress is made because you can't move toward a nonexistent end point.

If the Church is going to engage in a dialogue on any official, *corporate* level, then there needs to be the possibility of a *corporate* solution. By this I mean a true union between the parties. In Catholic theology, corporate union—true "full communion"—comes about through *Eucharistic* union. Only when parties can both share in a common Eucharist can they be truly united. The only instance in which this is possible is with the Eastern Orthodox churches. Only the Orthodox churches have valid sacraments and a valid hierarchy (and therefore a valid Eucharist), so only these churches can even theoretically be reunited with the Catholic Church at a corporate level. An official dialogue with them can be fruitful because it has a concrete end in mind: Eucharistic union.

Any such corporate reunion, however, is impossible with communities without a valid Eucharist, such as the Anglicans, all Protestant communities and, of course, all non-Christian religions. If Methodist leaders, for example, wanted to unite with Catholicism, there is no mechanism for the Methodist *church* to unite with the Catholic Church, since it has no valid Eucharist. All that is possible is for individual Methodists to become Catholics—and today's ecumenical dialogue actually discourages that. So it would be better for the Church—and more in keeping with her mission—to spend her energies working for individual conversions to Catholicism. The Gospel must be proclaimed to members of those communities as individuals.

Proclamation in place of dialogue does not mean that Catholics cannot or should not work together with non-Catholics for the common good (which, remember, is often the stated rationale for modern interreligious dialogue). However, the goals of these engagements should be specific and non-religious. A practical example of how this works well is the coalition of Catholics and non-Catholics working together to fight legalized abortion. For decades now Catholics and Evangelical Protestants have joined forces to push for pro-life initiatives. All parties focus on the single goal: fighting legalized abortion. Yet within the pro-life movement one rarely finds religious indifference. In fact, during pro-life events one often witnesses vigorous debate among the participants regarding their religious differences. This debate is honest, sincere, and direct. It was my involvement in the pro-life movement as an Evangelical Protestant that first led me to encounter dedicated Catholics, and it was through my engagement with them that I eventually converted to Catholicism. We did not engage in modern-day "dialogue," but forcefully sought the conversion of each other to what we believed to be the truth. Yet we were still able to work together for the common good of an end to abortion. Working together does not have to mean sweeping aside our differences.

If the Church is to regain her mission, the days of dialogue must be ended. Proclamation must again reign supreme.

The One True Church

As we've seen, for decades Church leaders and Catholic theologians have downplayed (or even denied) the uniqueness of Catholicism. Intentionally or not, this has caused many Catholics to believe that their Church is just one religious option among many. That must change. We need to regain some of the maligned "triumphalism" of our forefathers in the Faith, the conviction that the Catholic Church is the one true Church founded by Jesus Christ.

"Triumphalism," of course, is an insult conjured to imply that those who proclaim the uniqueness of Catholicism are somehow arrogant and lacking in Christian humility. But stating a truth — in this case, that the Catholic Church *is* the Church of Jesus Christ — is not an act of pride. In fact, humility always requires the recognition of reality. Catholics need not be embarrassed to state unequivocally that the Catholic Church is the one true religion and everyone needs to join her. As St. Paul wrote, "For I am not ashamed of the gospel; it is the power of God for salvation to every one who has faith" (Rom. 1:16). It is not prideful to proclaim the necessity of the Church, for it is only by grace that anyone becomes a member of her. Further, it is not due to the membership of any person that what the Church teaches is true. All these things are due to God alone.

Expression of the uniqueness of Catholicism is harmed by the Church's use of ambiguous language. Stating that the Church of Jesus Christ "subsists in" the Catholic Church, for example, sows confusion, not clarity. Whether it was the original drafter's intention or not, this phrase has been used to advance Religious Pluralism. By choosing the simple (and historic) language that the Church of Jesus Christ "is" the Catholic Church, we make plain that all who follow Christ should become Catholic. This language does not preclude the truth that certain bonds unite Catholics to other Christians, particularly the Eastern Orthodox.

We know that shifting the emphasis of language changed the beliefs of Catholics following the 1960s, so shifting the language back to more simple and traditional ways of speaking will help move the beliefs of Catholics away from Religious Pluralism and religious indifference. Insisting again that the Church of Christ *is* the Catholic Church will be a clear sign that being Catholic *matters*.

Beware of Errors

The third aspect of the Emphasis Shift was the move from warning against the errors of other religions to embracing our commonalities. On the surface, embracing commonalities seems like the most charitable way to interact with members of other religions because we assume warning against errors leads to conflict. Theoretically, avoiding verbal conflict will help us avoid the nastiness of religious wars, the Crusades, the Inquisition, etc.

However, warning against errors, even if it leads to conflict, is often the most charitable action a person can take. Think first of errors in the non-religious realm. If you're teaching your daughter how to drive and she has the turn signals reversed in her mind, you correct her error, even if she doesn't like to be corrected. You know it could harm her (or others) if she doesn't know the truth about how to use a turn signal. Likewise, if a friend is beginning to socialize with people you know to be drug users, you will warn him of the potential dangers of their company. It's possible that your friend will reject your warning—and your friendship—but if you love him, you want what is best for him. Conflict-avoidance doesn't trump true charity. If someone you love is following a harmful error, you try to correct him.

Now, everyone recognizes that misusing turn signals and hanging out with drug dealers is dangerous. Religious error is dangerous too—but the Emphasis Shift obscured that fact. In his 2020 encyclical *Fratelli Tutti*, Pope Francis placidly says of other religions, "Others drink from other sources."[228] From this, it sounds like all religions can equally supply fresh, life-giving water. But what about a religion like Islam that oppresses women in horrific ways and forces people to convert by the tip of the sword? What if following other religions leads not to life, but to death? The "water" of other religions often contains poison. Would it not be the most charitable action to at least inform them of the poison and urge them not to drink from that source?

Religious error can be far more dangerous than any disease or any poison or even any war. For religious error can lead not just to physical death and destruction, but to eternal damnation. "For what shall it profit a man, if he shall gain the whole world, and lose his own soul?" (Mark 8:36 KJV). The Church cannot put positive feelings of human fraternity above the need for spiritual health. When the Church ignores religious error, then, she commits spiritual malpractice.

Shifting Back

If Catholics begin to reverse the Emphasis Shift, how will our interactions with non-Catholics look? I detail many of the practical aspects of this in my book *The Old Evangelization*.[229] What do I mean by the "Old Evangelization"? Simply put, it is modeling our sharing the Faith today on the examples of Jesus and Catholic missionary saints. It means looking back at how the Catholic Faith was spread throughout the world historically, recognizing that while times and cultures change, people and their deepest

---

[228] Pope Francis, *Fratelli Tutti*, 277 (cf. chapter 18 of this book).
[229] Eric Sammons, *The Old Evangelization* (El Cajon, CA: Catholic Answers Press, 2017).

needs don't. People of all times are created with a desire to be united to truth and love, which is only found in Jesus Christ and His Church.

We can understand the Old Evangelization better by contrasting it with the aspects of the New Evangelization I discussed in chapter 20.

The New Evangelization is nonconfrontational. The Old Evangelization says it like it is, and it doesn't avoid the hard topics like Hell, divorce, or the errors of Islam.

The New Evangelization focuses on dialogue with the culture. The Old Evangelization recognizes the dangers inherent in modern culture and doesn't shy away from pointing those dangers out, while seeking to transform the culture with the light of the Gospel.

The New Evangelization focuses on fallen-away, nonpracticing Catholics. The Old Evangelization, while not ignoring those poor souls, casts a wide net, ambitiously seeking to convert to Catholicism every soul, even those serious about their (false) religions.

The New Evangelization de-emphasizes eternal consequences. The Old Evangelization recognizes that there is no greater tragedy than eternal damnation, and it isn't afraid to warn those who are in danger of this fate.

The New Evangelization employs a soft touch with non-Catholics. The Old Evangelization, desiring the salvation of all, isn't afraid to emphasize the ordinary means of salvation and to point out errors that lead people away from God, even if doing so does not lead to approbation.

As a practical example, let's look back at the exchange between Bishop Robert Barron and the Protestant Cameron Bertuzzi
that we detailed in chapter 20. Bertuzzi asked Bishop Barron,
"Should I become Catholic?" and we detailed Barron's "New
Evangelization" answer. What would the Old Evangelization
response to Bertuzzi's question be? I imagine it would be something like this:

"Should you become Catholic? Yes. Yes. A thousand times
yes! Absolutely you should become Catholic. There are two
main reasons why. The first is that the Catholic Church is
the Church of Jesus Christ; it is the Church that Jesus Christ
founded. And so to be a follower of Jesus Christ, you want to
be a member of His Church, the Body of Christ. In fact, the
early Church was so insistent on this point that it developed
the doctrine of 'outside the Church there is no salvation.' We
must be part of the Catholic Church in order to be united with
Christ here on earth but also in Heaven. And so we need to be
visible members of that Church in order to be faithful followers
of Jesus Christ.

"The second reason is because living as a Catholic here in
this world is the best way to live. It is the path to joy and happiness both in eternity and here on earth. This happens primarily
through living a sacramental life, which is only available through
the Church. Particularly in the sacraments of Confession and
Communion, we unite ourselves closer and closer to Christ each
day. After all, that is the goal of the Christian: to be united to
Christ. To be able to say, like St. Paul, 'It is no longer I who live,
but Christ who lives in me' (Gal. 2:20). And so therefore we want
to be members of the Catholic Church here on earth, because
that helps us to be more closely united to Christ here and one
day be united with Him completely in Heaven.

"Should you become Catholic? Yes. Yes, absolutely yes! It is the best decision that you could possibly make, and I guarantee you will not regret it."[230]

Nothing about an answer like this is obnoxious, overbearing, or offensive. Yet it makes it abundantly clear that the Protestant should become Catholic, and it doesn't bring up the extraordinary means of salvation, leaving those means to God. In essence, it prioritizes the Protestant's salvation over all other factors.

Ultimately, the foundation of reversing the Emphasis Shift and re-embracing the Old Evangelization is *love*. If you truly love someone, you want what is best for him. And there is nothing better for someone than union with Christ, both here on earth and in Heaven for eternity. To deny that gift to another out of fear of offending him or a desire to be considered relevant to the world, or for any other reason, is fundamentally an unloving act. For decades Catholics have been abandoning the Church, and fewer and fewer non-Catholics are coming into the Church. These are more than statistics; they are souls who were made to be with God. If we truly love them, then we will reverse the Emphasis Shift, abandon the failed New Evangelization, embrace the Old Evangelization, and seek the conversion of all people to the Catholic Church.

---

[230] A video of this answer can be found at https://www.facebook.com/ericrsammons/posts/3418594851697988.

24

Renewing the Parish

Although this book has looked closely at the teachings and actions of popes, bishops, and theologians, we're really interested in the impact of these things on the average Catholic: how has the Emphasis Shift—driven by leaders and theologians—influenced normal, pew-sitting Catholics? It is children raised by these average Catholics who will become the future priests, bishops, theologians, and lay people who will continue the mission of the Church. If we are to reclaim that mission, then we need to "reclaim" the average Catholic.

Nothing shapes the beliefs of regular Catholics more than their experience at their parish. It is at the parish that they come in direct contact with "the Church." For many Catholics, in fact, this is their *only* direct contact with Catholicism, and so how a parish presents the Faith has dramatic import for what a Catholic believes. If we are to reverse the Emphasis Shift and reclaim the Church's mission, parishes need renewal. How will this be achieved?

Parishes must take to heart the conclusions of the previous two chapters first of all. They must teach and live by an Exclusivist perspective on salvation, valuing water Baptism as God's ordinary means for salvation. Secondly the old methods of evangelization should be readopted so that the Faith may be proclaimed with love and fervor. Resting on that foundation, this chapter offers practical steps for parishes.

Much of the impetus for any change at the parish level rests with priests, staff, and volunteers who have varying levels of influence over how the parish is run. If you feel you have no such sway at your parish or that your parish decision-makers have no interest in change for the better, I suggest finding a parish that already practices these ideas to some extent.

Stick to the Mission

A parish must know its purpose: *the salvation of souls*. Many parishes create mission statements in order to communicate why they exist. Often these mission statements include declarations about the importance of celebrating the sacraments, serving the community, and being faithful stewards. Yet every parish should have a single mission statement: "To save souls." Every activity, no matter how involved or simple, should be undertaken in view of this one overriding goal. It's the only reason a parish exists.

When many parish activities are judged in the light of this basic mission, their value is called into question. For example, how does the interfaith service advance the salvation of souls? How does a book club that selects a book with anti-Catholic themes? (I know of a parish book club that read *The DaVinci Code*, and not in a critical way.) Does a parish's participation in a youth sports league that holds its games on Sundays really bring families along the path to salvation? Anything that doesn't foster the mission to save souls must be eliminated.

The singular mission to save souls does not preclude service or social activities. Instead it gives them focus and keeps them from moving away from this core mission. In my hometown, nearly every parish holds an annual summer "festival." Festivals typically include fair rides, lots of food and beer, kids' games, and gambling and games for adults. These festivals are major events in the community, with thousands of people, Catholics and non-Catholics, attending (at least before COVID-19). More importantly for the parish, they are major fundraisers, and most parishes depend heavily on them for their various programs and services.

Aside from fundraising, the justification for these festivals is that they help build community and give non-Catholics an easy way to connect with the local Catholic church. They are supposed to be wholesome ways to bring people together and to promote the parish. Yet in practice festivals more often turn people away from Catholicism than draw them to it. When I was a Protestant in high school, I looked upon these festivals as totally irreligious, even anti-religious, events. There was nothing distinctively Catholic about them. When I witnessed widespread drunkenness at festivals, it lowered my esteem for Catholicism. It did not seem like a serious religion to me, and I knew many other fervent Protestants who felt the same way, along with a small number of Catholics. One local faithful priest, in fact, began calling them "fest-evils" due to the sin they promoted. Catholic parishes continue to claim festivals are opportunities for people to get connected to their local parish and learn about Catholicism. But these festivals do not exist to save souls.

Getting sidetracked with community-building isn't the only way parishes stray from their purpose. All sorts of earthly rather than the spiritual pursuits present pitfalls. Many parishes, for example, devote their limited resources to popular social causes while worship and spiritual life suffers. Earth Day is sometimes more celebrated than All Saints' Day! Resources that could be spent encouraging devotions or catechesis are directed toward letter-writing campaigns and recycling programs. Getting heavily involved in political issues that are best left to the prudential judgments of the laity shifts the focus of parishioners from the eternal to the here-and-now.

This is not to say that Catholics shouldn't be involved in the betterment of our world. But an emphasis on the spiritual in parish life properly orders time and resources. Individual lay Catholics can of course organize or be involved in groups that work toward earthly goals, but parishes, which exist for the salvation of souls, should not. With millions of Catholics leaving, the Church is a little like a winless football team: Should we ponder our team deficiencies on the field, or what our vending machines should carry?

If a parish presses home the singular goal of saving souls, then it will be easy for parish leadership to see which events and activities obscure and even work against that goal. Community-building or social justice cannot be used as justification for an activity that strays from the parish's core mission. Every parish service and social activity should be measured with *saving souls* as the yardstick. What doesn't either directly or indirectly foster that mission should be dropped. Ecumenical or interreligious gatherings that foster indifference should be dropped. Sports leagues that fill the Lord's Day with the stress of driving around town to get to the next game should be eliminated. Festivals that encourage and entice people to sin are obviously no-goes. The programs that remain should be re-evaluated each year to ensure they don't drift from the heart of the parish's mission. "To save souls" must be the driving force of everything a parish does.

Speak Up

We noted in chapter 21 that rising religious indifference neutered many parishes' voices when it comes to controversial issues. However, these "hard" issues can directly impact a person's salvation, and so, in keeping with the underlying mission to save souls, these topics must be addressed.

Consider the topic of Hell. Although Jesus often spoke of eternal damnation, Hell is rarely, if ever, mentioned in a modern Catholic parish. One reason is a misguided belief that such talk will make people feel uncomfortable. Underlying the reticence to speak of Hell is also the assumption that very few people will go there, an assumption based on the Inclusivist move to make the extraordinary means of salvation ordinary. Yet if the mission of a parish is to save souls, then Hell *must* be mentioned frequently, because that's what souls are being saved from!

Is it true that people will leave the parish if topics like Hell (or contraception or divorce) are discussed? Sadly, yes. In today's society, even mentioning a hot topic like Hell is sure to turn some people off. Those who attend a parish for social reasons likely have little desire to hear about something that makes them squirm. And, since so many Catholics are religiously indifferent, the topic is considered an unnecessary relic of the past.

A parish's mission doesn't include keeping everyone happy and comfortable. A parish should not be tailored for the preferences of those people who are the least attached to the parish (and who are likely the most religiously indifferent members of the parish). Further, speaking hard truths cannot be restricted to the pulpit (although that is the primary place for it). Adult education should address these topics, as should children's education (in an age-appropriate way, of course). Parishioners should be trained in the methods of the Old Evangelization and encouraged to use them.

By speaking out on the "hard" topics, a parish will lose members. But many of those who remain will be impacted and will realize that being Catholic is more than just being part of a social club known as a "parish." They will become more serious about their faith. Compare a parish to an army training camp: Would you rather go to war with 2,000 flabby soldiers or 1,000 well-trained and physically fit soldiers?

Parishioners must be awakened from their religiously indifferent stupor. They will be faced with a choice, a choice that has possibly never been offered to them during decades of attending a Catholic parish: Do you choose Jesus Christ and His Church or not? Unless parishes address hard topics, they allow many Catholics to skate through their religious life without ever recognizing how serious the stakes are.

Change the Vibe

When a visitor walks into a typical Catholic parish today, what does he *feel*? In other words, what is the "vibe" of the parish? As I mentioned previously, all too often the overall ambience of the modern Catholic parish resembles that of a local community center. It is a place for people to gather and meet. Nothing about it boldly proclaims, "We believe Catholicism is the one true religion!" This atmosphere doesn't act only on visitors but on regular parishioners as well. It forms the way parishioners, perhaps subconsciously, view their faith. Though this "beige" aura is based in religious indifference, it also fosters it. In order to restore the Church's mission, we need to oust the beige. But how?

Two things that help determine the vibe of a parish are the art/architecture of the parish and how Mass is celebrated. And here again we will perceive that religious indifference has wreaked havoc on every aspect of modern Catholic life.

Consider the blandness of many Catholic church buildings. The Emphasis Shift cheerleaders led a drive to keep our parishes from not looking "too Catholic." The thinking was that parishes that were too historically Catholic-looking would be off-putting to non-Catholics. The result of this neutralizing influence has been to diminish Catholic identity and foster religious indifference. It quietly promotes the subconscious idea that there's nothing unique about Catholicism. When there is little difference between how the Catholic church and the Protestant church down the street look, it's easy for the churchgoers to believe that there is likely little difference between their religions.

Catholic churches should appear explicitly and unapologetically Catholic. Obviously the basic architecture of a church building cannot be easily changed (at least, not without great cost), but the interior can be. Parishes must give worship — not community building or education or other outreaches — the priority in resource allocation. This includes how churches are decorated, for that fosters proper worship. Statues of saints, a large crucifix, stained glass windows, and a prominent and beautiful tabernacle all contribute to the message that Catholicism is different from other religions (and felt banners do not).[231] People who enter should immediately think, "This is a *Catholic* church."

The way in which Mass is celebrated also contributes significantly to the feel of a parish. Part of the Emphasis Shift that was not covered in this book is the overhaul of the Mass that occurred in the 1960s (many books have already been written

---

[231] One resource to consider when redesigning the interior of a parish is Liturgical Arts Journal (www.liturgicalartsjournal.com/).

about this topic[232]). Part of the stated desire of the liturgical reformers was to make the Mass more palatable to Protestants; thus, many of the explicitly Catholic aspects of the Mass were either eliminated or toned down. The thinking was, as was the case with most of the Emphasis Shift, that by turning things down a notch the Church would attract more people. We've seen, of course, the opposite reaction. And again, when the Mass is made less distinctly Catholic, Catholics are left to wonder what makes Catholicism distinct.

A parish can't change the essentials of the Mass, of course, but it can change how it is celebrated. Here are a few suggestions. (Note: these suggestions are primarily for those parishes that celebrate the Ordinary Form of the Mass; the Extraordinary Form already has these features built in. Of course, only the parish priest has the authority to implement any of these suggestions.)

First, priests should consider celebrating the Mass *ad orientem*. This means "facing the East," and it signifies that the priest faces the altar during most of the Mass. *Ad orientem* has been maligned since the 1960s, with critics saying the priest is "turning his back to the people." But *ad orientem* powerfully shows that the priest is leading his people in worship and that they all face God together. Further, it is the historic way in which Mass is celebrated (and

---

[232] For a deeper understanding of the changes to the Mass in the 1960s, I recommend the following books: Peter Kwasniewski, *Reclaiming Our Roman Catholic Birthright: The Genius and Timeliness of the Traditional Latin Mass* (Brooklyn, NY: Angelico Press, 2020); Fr. James Jackson, *Nothing Superfluous* (Lincoln, NE: Redbrush, 2016); and Michael Fiedrowicz, *The Traditional Mass: History, Form, and Theology of the Classical Roman Rite* (Brooklyn, NY: Angelico Press, 2020).

it is how the Christian East has always celebrated—and still celebrates—its divine liturgy).

In addition to other arguments in its favor, *ad orientem* works in two ways to combat religious indifference. The first is that it helps distinguish Catholic worship from Protestant services. Since Protestant services are mostly focused on the relationship between the pastor and the congregation, they naturally involve the pastor speaking directly to the people. However, the Catholic Mass is primarily the worship of God, and so the "action" of the Mass is directed toward God—priest and people together. When the priest faces the altar it helps impress this reality on every person. This also reveals that the Catholic Mass is a fundamentally *different* form of worship than a Protestant service.

Another advantage of *ad orientem* is that it engenders *seriousness* in the worship. When a priest faces in the same direction as the people, it is easier to recognize that this is not just a meeting led by a presider. It is the worship of the Almighty God of the Universe. There is no greater enemy of religious indifference than religious seriousness, for it forces people into a choice: Do you think the practice of religion is the most important thing in your life, or is it just an activity you do from time to time? Seriousness elevates the practice of religion and distinguishes it from other activities in life. A person who takes his religion seriously can't help but believe that his religion is different from other religions.

Another suggestion for changing how the Mass is celebrated is the choice of music. Perhaps nothing is more of a "third rail" for pastors than what music is sung at Mass. Everyone has his opinion, and it seems that no one is ever completely happy. Yet that should not dissuade a parish's leadership from recognizing that the music sung at Mass can foster religious indifference, arising from both its lyrics and its composition.

In one survey of American Catholics,[233] the three most popular hymns were, "Be Not Afraid," "Here I Am, Lord," and "On Eagle's Wings." There is nothing distinctively Catholic about the lyrics in any of these songs; in fact, there is nothing distinctively *Christian* about the lyrics. The songs could be sung at a Catholic Mass, a Protestant service, or even at a Jewish synagogue. Further, the fourth-most popular hymn, "Amazing Grace," was written by a Protestant and is one of the most popular songs used in Protestant services. So, what are currently our most popular hymns fail to convey the distinctiveness of Catholicism.

And it's not just the lyrics that foster indifference. Since the Emphasis Shift, most Catholic musicians strive to make Catholic music as "relevant" as possible. In other words, the type of music people hear at Mass should be as similar as possible to what they hear outside of Mass. The argument is that this type of music is more attractive to modern ears, particularly younger ones, and so using this music will make the Mass more attractive. However, in practice this makes the Mass less distinctive, and it therefore seems less important.

The Catholic Church has a long history of beautiful music in the Mass, particularly the development of Gregorian Chant (which Vatican II said should be "given pride of place in liturgical services"[234]). This music is distinctively Catholic. When a Hollywood director wants to make a scene in a movie feel "Catholic," he doesn't choose a 1970s ditty like "On Eagle's Wings" as background music; he chooses a Gregorian Chant or

---

[233] Isabelle Senechal, "The Greatest Hymns of All Time (as chosen by America readers)," *America*, October 2, 2019, https://www.americamagazine.org/faith/2019/10/02/greatest-hymns-all-time-chosen-america-readers.

[234] *Sacrosanctum Concilium*, 116.

some other classic Catholic hymn. If secular Hollywood direc-
tors understand this, so should pastors: if you want to make your
parish feel Catholic, then sing traditionally Catholic hymns.

A final practical suggestion for combating religious indifference in a parish is *silence*. Specifically, silence before and after
Mass in the nave of the church. Why silence? Like *ad orientem*
worship, silence projects seriousness. Consider the difference
between walking into a church where most people are chatting about their week versus one where it is quiet and people
are silently praying. In the latter atmosphere it is clear that the
people there believe something significant is about to happen.
This aura says Catholicism *matters*, and that's the antidote for
religious indifference.

Renewing the Church — One Parish at a Time

Parishes are the frontlines of the Church: they are where Catholics have their most direct interaction with the Catholic Faith.
Because the Emphasis Shift caused religious indifference to creep
into parishes, many are little different from community centers. If
we want to reclaim the Church's mission and convert the world
to Catholicism, parishes must reverse the Emphasis Shift and
embrace an unapologetically and distinctively Catholic way of
doing things, from what activities they offer to how they worship
to how they look and feel. This chapter explored a few of the
ways to do this, but if change proves impossible at your parish,
find a parish where it's not.

It may appear from this chapter that I wish to take away all
the events that make a parish interesting or enjoyable. That is not
the case. A parish that boldly proclaims the truth and prioritizes
fostering the spiritual life will be far more "vibrant" than the
parishes who lay claim to being vibrant now based on the number

of activities they offer. But it is true that parishes will likely need to severely limit or eliminate many of their current offerings. If a person contracts a serious disease, he goes to the hospital to focus on recovering; he does not go to Disneyland. Parishes are sick today. They must concentrate on recovery before anything else. Perhaps when (Lord willing) the Church has recovered her mission, parishes can offer more diverse activities.

The Church will be renewed one parish at a time. And the way to do this is by making parishes once again waystations on the path to salvation, rather than community organizations stuck on the merry-go-round of this world.

Conclusion

Many times in the New Testament we find the Church called the Bride of Christ (Rev. 21:2; cf. 2 Cor. 11:2, Eph. 5:21-33). Our Lord the loving Bridegroom lavishes wonderful gifts on her. Adorned in gold and jewels, she possesses a beauty that shines forth by virtue of His gifts. Recently, however, the Bride has had her head turned. She has become besotted with cheap trinkets and gaudy jewelry. She has forgotten her royal standing.

Christ gave the Church a mission: "Go therefore and make disciples of all nations, baptizing them in the name of the Father and of the Son and of the Holy Spirit, teaching them to observe all that I have commanded you" (Matt. 28:19-20). For the salvation of all people, He instituted the Church, and to her alone He entrusted the road to salvation. Yet in recent years she has cast aside this privilege, becoming more like just another woman on the street than the Bride of the King.

Because the Church has abdicated her mission, millions of people have left, and countless souls who may have otherwise become Catholic failed to do so. Most Catholics who remain have embraced the belief that there is nothing unique — nothing royal — about the Church. The beauty of the Bride has been hidden.

The blame for this tragedy lies with the Emphasis Shift that originated in the 1960s. For almost two millennia the Church knew and lived her unique mission, but then she abruptly turned her eyes to all the possible ways one could be saved without her. The consequences devastated our outreach to others and the faith of many Catholics.

Imagine the following scenario. Three people are chatting in the living room when a fire breaks out in the kitchen. The first person, Peter Pluralist, is convinced that water isn't necessary to put out the fire and gasoline will work just as well. He grabs a nearby gas can and heads for the kitchen. The second, Irene Inclusivist, knows that water is needed but doesn't say anything to Peter. She doesn't like correcting people and hopes the fire will go out on its own. The third person, Evan Exclusivist, quickly finds water, rushes to the kitchen, stops Peter, and puts out the fire. In this situation, Peter was wrong and dangerous, and Irene was right but did nothing to squelch the fire, while Evan was both right and helpful.

Right now, millions of souls are in more danger than that hypothetical kitchen. Yet the only possessor of spiritual water, the Catholic Church, has been behaving like Irene or Peter, withholding the means for putting out the spiritually damaging fires. Instead of preaching about the life-giving waters of Christ, she looks for all the other ways a fire could in theory be extinguished. Because of this, many souls are being lost and the Church has neglected her mission to save them. It gives new meaning to the phrase "Hell's Kitchen."

Now is the time to turn back and reclaim the Church's mission. It is imperative that we restore the foundations of the Church's true message. We must reverse the Emphasis Shift and again proclaim the Church as the ordinary means of salvation.

Will reversing course mean going back to exactly how things were before the Emphasis Shift? It shouldn't. The world has changed, and we will find new ways to preach the Gospel (rather than finding a new Gospel to preach). How that looks may be different now than it was in 1920. However, adapting to modern times cannot mean abandoning the foundation of the Church's mission. Sixty years of doing so has wreaked havoc.

There is hope. Even when the Church has forgotten her mission, Christ has not forgotten her. By recognizing what we have lost, Catholics can again make the Church the light that shines in this dark world. She is the ark of salvation. Let's first be sure we're on that ark and then bring as many people as possible on board.

Appendix A

Can Catholics Criticize Popes and Councils?

Millions of people have left Catholicism over the past few decades, and the Church has had an increasingly waning influence on the world. All indications are that these trends will continue. The Church, the Bride of Christ, is sick.

When you are sick and go to the doctor, it's normal to be asked standard questions about your life: What is your diet? How often do you exercise? Do you smoke? These questions aren't asked to make you feel guilty about bad decisions; they are a way of uncovering clues about your illness. Our past choices are often the key to our present condition.

Likewise, if the Church is currently sick, as I believe she is, we cannot go about curing her without knowing what made her sick. This means we have to look unblinkingly at our past, especially our recent past. We have to recognize where Church leaders have made mistakes. These mistakes might entail imprudent decisions, watering down of Church teaching, or even the promotion of erroneous doctrines. Sweeping these decisions under the rug doesn't do the Church any good, just as hiding from the doctor the fact that you're a smoker doesn't help you in the long run.

This is difficult for any organization, but it's particularly a challenge for Catholics. We believe that the Church is led by the Holy Spirit and that her official teachings regarding theology and morality are infallible—without error. We also believe that the Church is a hierarchy, and, as such, those on the lower rungs of the ladder—lay people especially—are to follow the decisions of those on the higher rungs, such as the bishops and the pope. So, does that mean a criticizing Catholic is automatically a bad Catholic?

I hope not, since in this book I've directed a good deal of criticism at popes and bishops. I do not believe that makes me a bad Catholic, however, for the Church has never taught that Church leaders are above criticism.

Church leaders have been criticized for their actions since the very beginnings of the Church. In his Letter to the Galatians, St. Paul tells of his opposition to St. Peter, the first pope. Peter refused to have fellowship with Gentile converts for fear of offending members of a strict group of Christians. Paul writes, "But when Cephas [Peter] came to Antioch I opposed him to his face, because he stood condemned" (Gal. 2:11). Out of human weakness Peter had made an imprudent decision, and Paul knew that Peter's actions caused scandal and division in the Church, harming her long-term mission of saving souls. So he publicly corrected Peter, even though Peter was the acknowledged head of the Church. This incident makes clear that it is acceptable to criticize Church leaders when their actions call for it.

How do we distinguish, though, situations in which Church leaders can be criticized versus those comprising infallible teachings that must be followed? We know that Catholics believe Church leaders can declare things infallibly, that is, without error. These declarations are most commonly made either by the pope alone or in an ecumenical council, which is a worldwide gathering of bishops united to the pope. Obviously, criticizing something that has been declared without error (infallibly) is a losing proposition for any Catholic. It's unthinkable. A Catholic cannot deny the Immaculate Conception or say the Church is wrong about transubstantiation and still be a Catholic in good standing. So does this mean that popes and councils can never be criticized?

Criticizing Councils

Let's first consider ecumenical councils. This is important because an ecumenical council has a starring role in this book: the Second Vatican Council, held from 1962-1965. Vatican II was the twenty-first ecumenical council of the Catholic Church. Ecumenical councils make declarations about Catholic teaching as well as recommendations regarding Catholic pastoral practices. Often councils are held in times of great crisis—to address a popular heresy or confront scandals within the Church. When Pope John XXIII called Vatican II in 1959, many were surprised, since most believed that the Church was facing no obvious crisis. John XXIII said he called the council to meet "the spiritual needs of the present time." He wanted to help the Church better interact with the modern world.

Every ecumenical council has some impact on the Church of her times, some more than others. In the case of Vatican II, its impact on the Church cannot be overestimated: it has influenced every aspect of the Church and parish life today, from how we receive the sacraments, to what music we sing at Mass, to how our children are catechized, to how we view other religions. Can the changes that occurred due to Vatican II be criticized? Are Catholics to believe that every word from a council should be treated as an utterance of the Holy Spirit?

As already mentioned, ecumenical councils are one way in which the Church practices her charism of infallibility. But the charism of infallibility encompasses only specific dogmatic statements, and so it does not extend to every act and every statement of an ecumenical council. Councils are not convened only to make dogmatic declarations, i.e., pronouncements on faith and morals. Often, their intention is to create or modify existing *disciplines* within the Church or to offer *pastoral guidance* on pressing issues of the day. Examples of disciplines include the prayers said during liturgical celebrations or the rules for how a bishop administers his diocese. Pastoral guidance might include how missionary priests engage with non-Christian peoples or suggestions on how to be involved in the political sphere.

Disciplines and pastoral guidance may change over time because they are bound to particular times and circumstances. Further, since these are not dogmatic declarations, there is no divine protection attached to them: councils can at times issue imprudent disciplines or poor guidance. Only when a council intends to define a doctrine in faith or morals for all the Church to believe is it protected by the Holy Spirit.

So, did Vatican II make any such infallible declarations? According to the man who was pope for most of Vatican II, Paul VI, it did not:

> There are those who ask what authority, what theological qualification the Council intended to give to its teachings, knowing that it avoided issuing solemn dogmatic definitions engaging the infallibility of the ecclesiastical Magisterium. The answer is known by whoever remembers the conciliar declaration of March 6, 1964, repeated on November 16, 1964: given the Council's pastoral

character, *it avoided pronouncing, in an extraordinary manner, dogmas endowed with the note of infallibility.*[235]

Paul VI is saying here that the purpose of Vatican II was to issue disciplines and pastoral guidance, not to make dogmatic declarations. So we clearly see that Vatican II, while being a valid ecumenical council, did not make any new infallible pronouncements; thus, the disciplines it issued and the pastoral guidance it gave are not infallible and are open to criticism, especially in light of what occurred in the wake of Vatican II. To criticize Vatican II, therefore, is not to criticize the Holy Spirit, but instead to criticize fallible men, even while acknowledging that many of them made their decisions with the best of intentions. Unfortunately, good intentions are not always enough to guarantee a good outcome.

Criticizing Popes

So what about popes? If councils can be criticized, does this mean popes can be criticized, too? The same basic logic applies. Popes are infallible only when they define a doctrine on faith or morals for the whole Church to believe. Everything else they say and do is at least *open* to criticism. We saw that St. Paul publicly opposed St. Peter when the head Apostle allowed weakness to compromise the proclamation of the Gospel. Another example from history is the case of Pope John XXII in the fourteenth century. He argued in his sermons that those who died in faith did not see the Beatific Vision until after the Last Judgment. The theology faculty at the University of Paris publicly criticized John, and eventually the pope recanted his error.

[235] Pope Paul VI, *General Audience*, January 12, 1966, emphasis added.

The Church has consistently taught that criticizing pastors, including the pope, is not off-limits to the faithful. St. Thomas Aquinas wrote, "if the faith were endangered, a subject ought to rebuke his prelate even publicly."[236] The *Catechism of the Catholic Church* confirms this teaching:

> In accord with the knowledge, competence, and pre-eminence which they possess, [lay people] have the right and even at times a duty to manifest to the sacred pastors their opinion on matters which pertain to the good of the Church, and they have a right to make their opinion known to the other Christian faithful, with due regard to the integrity of faith and morals and reverence toward their pastors, and with consideration for the common good and the dignity of persons. (CCC 907, cf. CIC 212 § 3).

This is an important lesson for us: popes are men with the same weaknesses and failings as any other men. When we look at the history of the Church, we see many saintly and good popes, but we also see scoundrels and weak, immoral men—and everything between.

Further, as men, popes do not have full knowledge, which means they can make decisions with the best of intentions that in the end have bad consequences. Say a mother sends her son to a well-respected school so he may receive a great education, but that school ends up having a terrible influence on his life. Although the mother had good intentions, her decision was negative in the long run for her son. A pope, likewise, might make a decision he believes will help his flock but that ultimately

---

[236] Aquinas, *Summa Theologica* II-II, q. 33, art. 4.

proves gravely harmful. Often this is only evident in hindsight. To pretend his decision was a good one is to ignore its negative consequences—and hinder the resolution of the problems resulting from that decision.

Note that even popes who are canonized saints can be criticized. When the Church canonizes a pope, or anyone for that matter, she is saying that this person is in Heaven and is a worthy model to emulate. The Church is *not* saying that the saint made no prudential mistakes or administration errors during his lifetime. Holiness does not protect one from human error.

That being said, it's also not healthy to have a constantly critical spirit. Any criticism a Catholic levels against a pope or a council should be offered carefully and in humility. No one *wants* to criticize his mother; he wants the world always to be like it was when he was a young child, where mom was always right and all-knowing. Yet that's not realistic in this fallen world.

We should not enjoy criticizing Church leaders, but we must do so at times in order that the Church may fulfill her glorious mission.

Appendix B

U.S. Catholic Statistics — 1970-2019

All statistics are from the Center for Applied Research in the Apostolate ("Frequently Requested Church Statistics").

Infant Baptisms (Previous Year): 46.5 Percent Decline

Year	Baptisms
1970	1.089 million
1975	894,992
1980	943,632
1985	953,323
1990	986,308
1995	981,444
2000	996,199
2005	929,545
2010	806,138

Year	Baptisms
2015	693,914
2019	582,331

Total Number of Priests: 39.3 Percent Decline

Year	Priests
1970	59,192
1975	58,909
1980	58,398
1985	57,317
1990	52,124
1995	49,054
2000	45,699
2005	41,399
2010	39,993
2015	37,578
2019	35,929

Total Number of Religious Sisters: 73.6 Percent Decline

Year	Sisters
1970	160,931
1975	135,225
1980	126,517
1985	115,386
1990	102,504
1995	90,809
2000	79,814
2005	68,634
2010	57,544
2015	48,546
2019	42,441

Marriages (Previous Year): 67.7 Percent Decline

Year	Marriages
1970	426,309
1975	369,133
1980	350,745

Year	Marriages
1985	348,300
1990	326,079
1995	294,144
2000	261,626
2005	207,112
2010	168,400
2015	148,134
2019	137,885

Percent of Catholics Who Attend Mass Every Week: 61.6 Percent Decline

Year	Percent Who Attend Mass
1970	54.9
1975	42
1980	42.2
1985	39.9
1990	32.5

U.S. Catholic Statistics — 1970-2019

Year	Percent Who Attend Mass
1995	26.4
2000	30.8
2005	25.6
2010	24.2
2015	23.4
2019	21.1

About the Author

Eric Sammons is the editor in chief of *Crisis Magazine* and the author of several books, including *The Old Evangelization: How to Spread the Faith Like Jesus Did* (Catholic Answers Press) and a high school textbook on ecumenism and interreligious dialogue. He holds a degree in systems analysis with a concentration in economics from Miami University in Ohio, where he was received into the Catholic Church in 1993. He earned a master of theology degree from Franciscan University and has worked for decades in Catholic evangelization at the individual, parish, and diocesan levels.

Eric and his wife, Suzan, have seven children and live in Ohio.

A special thanks to our *Deadly Indifference* launch team, who read this book before publication and helped us with promotion. Thank you for your time, input, and enthusiasm.

R.E. Anderson, Anthony Angelo, Carlos Arias, Anna Armstrong, Phil Barhorst, Matt Barhorst, Duane M. Barth, Margo Basso, Ryan Beggy, Phillip A. Bellini, Thomas Berryhill, Charles Blankenship, Aleksandra Blaszczyk, Terrence Boudreau, Donna M. Bungo, Aaron Carrico, Zachary Corbett, Peter Doane, Johann du Toit, Amanda Farnum, Gail Finke, Colman Fitzgerald, Andrew Flattery, David Furst, Matt Gaspers, Sergio Gonzalez, Francisco Green, Pamela Grothaus, Jacob Gunter, Kennedy Hall, Paul Hammond, Christine Harrington, Steve Hyatt, Edward Jacko, O.P., John and Colette Janney, Dr. Randy Juanta, Austen Kalin, Andy Katherman, Lucy Kildow, Louise Le Mottee, Melissa Linscomb, Derya Little, Elizabeth MacAdams, Fr. Matthew MacDonald, James Mahon, Vincent Marcantonio, Mike McCartney, Steven R. McEvoy, Tricia McKenna, Bob Merrill, Dan Millette, Sara Molloy, James Lee Murphy, Neil Newcomb, Carol Osteen, Laura Pardo, Paco Pepe Pérez Valero, Marla Perry, Denise Kibbe Phillips, Mario J. Prince, Daniel Quigley, Guillermo Ramos, Rudy Anthony Reyes, Maria Ring, Colleen Roca, Biff Rocha, Robert Roetting, Tyler Rowley, Gonzalo Ruiz-Esquide, Maryanne E. Santelli, Austin Sarabia, Harry Scherer, Joshua Schmidt, William and Gloria Schrader, Don Schwab, O.F.S., Fred Simon, Nick Spicher, Pawel Statuch, Alex Sullivan, Corey Swope, Jake Tate, Joseph Taylor, Michael Thomas, James Tiedemann, Fr. Sean M. Timmerman, Curtis Voeltner, Jim Walsh, Gary Wiley, Ryan Williams, David Wills, David Wilson, Tres Wolfford, Donna Woolston, Elizabeth Ann Wright, Erick Ybarra

CRISIS Publications

Sophia Institute Press awards the privileged title "CRISIS Publications" to a select few of our books that address contemporary issues at the intersection of politics, culture, and the Church with clarity, cogency, and force and that are also destined to become all-time classics.

CRISIS Publications are *direct*, explaining their principles briefly, simply, and clearly to Catholics in the pews, on whom the future of the Church depends. The time for ambiguity or confusion is long past.

CRISIS Publications are *contemporary*, born of our own time and circumstances and intended to become significant statements in current debates, statements that serious Catholics cannot ignore, regardless of their prior views.

CRISIS Publications are *classical*, addressing themes and enunciating principles that are valid for all ages and cultures. Readers will turn to them time and again for guidance in other days and different circumstances.

CRISIS Publications are *spirited*, entering contemporary debates with gusto to clarify issues and demonstrate how those issues can be resolved in a way that enlivens souls and the Church.

We welcome engagement with our readers on current and future CRISIS Publications. Please pray that this imprint may help to resolve the crises embroiling our Church and society today.